MEASURING TIME,
MAKING HISTORY

The Natalie Zemon Davis Annual Lecture Series

at Central European University, Budapest

MEASURING TIME, MAKING HISTORY

Lynn Hunt

Central European University Press

Budapest–New York

© 2008 by Lynn Hunt

Published in 2008 by

Design by Péter Tóth

Central European University Press
An imprint of the
Central European University Share Company
Nádor utca 11, H-1051 Budapest, Hungary
Tel: +36-1-327-3138 or 327-3000
Fax: +36-1-327-3183
E-mail: ceupress@ceu.hu
Website: www.ceupress.com

400 West 59th Street, New York NY 10019, USA
Tel: +1-212-547-6932
Fax: +1-646-557-2416
E-mail: mgreenwald@sorosny.org

ISBN 978-615-5211-48-5
ISSN 1996-1197

Library of Congress Cataloging-in-Publication Data
Hunt, Lynn Avery.
Measuring time, making history / Lynn Hunt. p. cm.
"Natalie Zemon Davis annual lecture series at Central European University,
Budapest"--Half t.p.
Lectures presented in Nov. 2006.
ISBN 978-9639776142 (pbk. : alk. paper)
1. History--Philosophy. 2. Time--Philosophy. I. Title.

D16.9.H88 2007   901--dc22   2007039301

Printed in Hungary by Akadémia Nyomda, Martonvásár

Contents

Preface and Acknowledgements

The Natalie Zemon Davis annual lectures at the Central European University provided the occasion for developing the ideas in this book. It was a great honor for me to be asked to give those lectures in November 2006. Natalie Davis is not only an immensely distinguished historian but also a mentor and example for many of us. She was my senior colleague at the University of California, Berkeley when I was fortunate enough to be hired there in 1974 for my first regular university position. I will never forget my anticipation at meeting her during my interview for the job or the many kindnesses she extended to me while we were colleagues. The time was not long before she went off to Princeton University, but it was

1

an intensely formative time for the young historian that I was then. Natalie brought a unique blend of charisma, enthusiasm, and good sense to the study and teaching of history, and she has as a consequence helped shape whole generations of young historians in the United States, Canada, and in many other places in the world as well.

One special place for her was the Central European University, and so I was thrilled to have the chance to follow in her footsteps there. I want to thank Gábor Klaniczay and his colleagues in the Medieval Studies Department and the History Department for their warm welcome, for the delightful introduction to the Central European University and the city of Budapest, and for their intellectual engagement with the themes I proposed. I want to thank as well the wonderful graduate students of the two departments who asked so many thoughtful and provocative questions at the lectures, thereby helping me to clarify my thoughts on the question of time and history.

Chapter 1
Is Time Historical?

"Time grows dim. Time that was so long
grows short, time, all goggle-eyed,
wiggling her skirts, singing her torch song,
giving the boys a buzz and a ride,
that Nazi Mama with her beer and sauerkraut.
Time, old gal of mine, will soon dim out."
Anne Sexton, First stanza of
"For Mr. Death Who Stands with His Door Open" (1974)

Time, as Sexton's lines so forcibly remind us, requires metaphor. It flows like a river, accelerates like an engine, flies like a winged chariot, freezes like instant ice, stands still like a heart between beats, or, in Sexton's words, grows short, and then dims out as death opens his door. Without the metaphors, whether "that Nazi Mama" wiggling her skirts, or the more venerable arrow of time, the fourth dimension would be exceedingly difficult to grasp. Linguists have noted that it is virtually impossible to talk about time without invoking motion (wiggling skirts, engines, chariots, arrows) and spatial content (short, long). A clock face, for instance, provides both motion, the moving hand, and spatial content, the space traversed by the hand. Even more modern conceptions of time seem to require spatial representation, however non-intuitive, as in, for example, the warping of space–time around black holes. In the post-Einstein world, space–time or the spacetime continuum (the combination of the two concepts, space and time, helps make the point) is most often described as a rubber sheet and the earth, for instance, as a marble whose roll across the rubber sheet slightly puckers the fabric. Again, we have motion and spatial content.[1]

Time feels like an essential and defining feature of human life, yet, when pressed to define it, we inevitably fall back upon duration, change, and ultimately, the tenses of our languages, past, present, and future. We all have a direct experience of time, or so we think, and yet it is the dimension of our lives about which there is the greatest philosophical and cosmological disagreement. Aristotle cut to the quick in his *Physics* (Book IV, ch. or part 10): "First, does it belong to the class of things that exist or to that of things that do not exist? Then secondly, what is its nature?" Is time real, in other words, or is it some kind of figment of the human imagination? Is time absolute, as Newton proposed, or relative, as Einstein argued?[2]

I do not pretend to resolve these enduring philosophical or cosmological dilemmas. Instead, I want to explore some of the ways in which time matters or should matter to historians. Like everyone else, historians assume that time exists, yet despite its obvious importance to historical writing—what is history but the account of how things change over time?—writers of history do not often inquire into the meaning of time itself. In the following pages I will ask a series of related questions about time in history. Why is time now again on the agenda, for historians and more generally in Western culture? Do the debates about the nature of time have particular implications for historians? How did Western Christian culture develop its distinctive way of measuring time (BC/AD or BCE/CE) and how does it influence our notion of history? What is the role of modernity—our most contentious temporal category—in the historical discipline? Is modernity an experience of temporality or an ideological construction? Are modernity, the discipline of history, and even the notion of history itself a western, and therefore imperialist, impositions? Should we, can we, move beyond the modern within the historical discipline?

WHEN TIME BECOMES URGENT

Although time is always with us, it becomes a subject of widespread concern only at certain moments. The most striking examples are the millennia in Western history, 1000 and 2000 AD. We still remember the world-wide worries, largely unfounded, about the supposed Y2K bug; because most computers used two digits rather than four for representing years, many feared that the coming of January 1, 2000 would lead to a global computer breakdown. Companies, governments, universities, and individuals paid out billions of dollars preparing for the changeover, which for the most part occurred without incident. The year 1000 was less precise in every way. For many years historians downplayed the once presumed apocalyptic millennialism of the year 1000 as a fantasy of romantic historians like Jules Michelet, but exactly 1000 years later, Richard Landes made a valiant effort to revive it, arguing that more recent historians have overlooked persuasive evidence of the phenomenon, especially in France. Despite the efforts of Augustine and the church hierarchy to suppress expectations of an imminent doomsday, popular apocalyptic prophets appeared repeatedly with claims to have received letters or other signs from heaven of the approaching end of time.[3]

Preachers of looming apocalypse emerged so often because the dating of the millennium was so uncertain. Much depended on the assignment of an age to the world since those who believed in an imminent end to it usually calculated the end from their dating of the world's beginning. According to some influential ecclesiastics of the early second century, a day in the eyes of God was equivalent to 1000 years. The passage in the Bible comes from 2 Peter 3:8, "one day [is] with the Lord as a thousand years, and a thousand years as one day." Therefore the Second Coming would only occur when the world was 6,000 years old (after the sixth day). Church historians of the early third century believed that the world was then 5,700 years old and therefore still three centuries away from the millennium. As 500 AD approached, however, churchmen recalculated the age of the world and moved the 6,000 year mark to 801 AD and then to 1000 AD.

Dating systems can still arouse controversy, especially when they are lifted out of the depths of common sense understanding into the harsh light of expli-

7

*- marking time is not uniform
or mutual; can be contintiaus*

cit discussion. The ongoing debate in the Anglophone world over BCE/CE versus BC/AD can be taken as a sign, in itself, of growing concern with or uncertainty about time. Many textbooks in the United States have adopted BCE/CE [Before the Common Era/Common Era] because it is deemed less insistently Christian and less elitist (not having the Latin basis of AD, *Anno Domini*, or year of the Lord). Some have vehemently resisted the change. In June 2000 the Southern Baptist Convention meeting in Orlando, Florida approved a resolution "On Retaining The Traditional Method Of Calendar Dating." It stated that "This practice [the use of BCE/CE] is the result of the secularization, anti-supernaturalism, religious pluralism, and political correctness pervasive in our society." The resolution is a good reminder that the means of marking time are still far from neutral.[4]

Whereas medieval time seems thoroughly imbued with religious meanings and issues, modern time appears more linked to technology, not least the diffusion of ever more precise and individual time pieces. Yet the distinction should not be exaggerated, for time continues to have a religious dimension—witness the Southern Baptists of today—and always had a technological one as well. The measurement of time requires technology of some sort. Yet, there is no denying that time becomes more technological from the seventeenth century onward. The moment that Christiaan Huygens invented the pendulum clock (ca 1657) might be taken as signaling this gathering momentum of technology. The drive to measure time more accurately became increasingly closely associated with mechanical science, with instrument making, and eventually with the individualization of timekeeping. Pocket watches, alarm clocks, and time cards to measure work would not be far behind.[5]

The intertwining of time and technology might be traced in any historical period, but the one that has drawn the most sustained attention of late is the fin-de-siècle of the twenty or thirty years preceding World War I. The very term, *end of the century*, draws attention to the special sense of time in that era. Should not every century have its "fin-de-siècle"? So why should this particular one be enshrined as such? Stephen Kern excavated that fin-de-siècle in his wide-ranging book, *The Culture of Time and Space, 1880–1918* (1983). Kern argues that "a series of sweeping changes in technology and culture created distinctive new modes of thinking about and experiencing time and space." Neither the sense of the past nor the sense of the future changed all that much, Kern maintains, but the sense of the present was "distinctively new, thickened temporally with retentions and protentions of past and future and, most important, expanded spatially to create the vast, shared experience of simultaneity," in part due to the introduction of World Standard Time in 1884.[6]

It is hard for us now to imagine the interest generated, for example, by the International Conference on Time held in Paris in 1912. The conference established a system for determining and transmitting accurate time signals. The French hosted the conference in order to make up for their previous tardiness: they did not adopt the Greenwich world standard, proposed in 1884, until 1911. In 1884 an international conference in Washington D.C. had divided the globe into twenty-four time zones and declared Greenwich, England the prime meridian (for time) because three-quarters of the world's shippers already used Greenwich as the 0 degree in longitude. Germany adopted the new standard in 1893, in part to facilitate military mobilization. Until 1911, however, Paris time was nine minutes and twenty-one seconds ahead of Greenwich time. In an effort to safeguard national primacy, the 1911 French law declared that "the legal time in France and Algeria is the mean Paris time slowed nine minutes and twenty-one seconds."[7]

Kern attributed the fin-de-siècle preoccupation with time to a combination of technological innovations—the telephone, wireless telegraph, x-ray, cinema, and the bicycle, automobile and airplane—and cultural ones, in particular the "affirmation of private time" with its radical interiority of experience, from the philosophy of Henri Bergson to the novels of Marcel Proust and James Joyce. In fact, however, the movement for World Standard Time got its biggest push from the railroads, which were hardly new at the end of the nineteenth century. They had by then reached the point of density at which coordination was becoming a necessity. In 1883, the railroad companies in the United States agreed to a four zone time system divided along the 75th, 90th, and 105th meridian lines. This agreement opened the way to the imposition of a world standard.[8]

Another such epoch of general concern with time seems to be upon us now, perhaps as a result of a similar kind of concatenation of technological and cultural causes. From the hard sciences to popular culture, time is on the agenda. In a recent special issue of *Daedalus* on time (Spring, 2003), a biologist claimed that specialists in fields as diverse as neuroscience and evolutionary biology now "regard the issue of time as urgent and inescapable"—albeit very different dimensions of time, milliseconds for neuroscientists and billions of years for evolutionary biologists. Circadian rhythms are the subject of intense research because they offer a way of linking processes across insects and mammals and perhaps eventually even plants and fungi; animals, plants, and fungi all have clock genes, which may have a common evolutionary origin.[9]

In physics, too, time raises many interesting, and still intractable, issues. Paul Steinhardt has argued that physics has three basic cosmic paradigms with different versions of time. The first, the Steady State Model, has been discarded because of the discovery of the expansion of the universe, but two remain in play—the Created Universe of Big Bang Theory in which time begins at the big bang and proceeds from there, and the Cyclic Universe in which space and time exist forever, alternately expanding and contracting. Understanding the role of time in gravity and in quantum theory appears to be crucial to the development of a general unified theory in physics; for some, gravity is none other than the unequal flow of time from place to place. Lurking beneath these discussions is the vexed problem of time's "arrow" or the direction of time in physics. We experience life as directional; we grow old, hot water grows cold, and the second law of thermodynamics (that entropy in systems increases over time) appears to explain this state of affairs. Yet most of the fundamental laws of physics imply reversibility, not directionality. So is time travel possible? Can we move backwards in time as well as forwards?[10]

Concern with time is not limited to the sciences. It permeates popular culture, from American TV programs such as "24," which purports to take place in real time (each episode covers an hour), to the Slow Food movement founded by an Italian to counteract Fast Food, through the constant newspaper and magazine articles about our lack of time. In social and political theory, the acceleration of time is now taken more or less for granted as an essential, if not defining, element of modern life, if not modernity itself. Hartmut Rosa has argued, for example, that "the history of modernity is an ongoing process of social acceleration," and he has set out to develop "a new critical theory of acceleration." Though Rosa posits acceleration as an ongoing process, it seems significant that his work has only come to widespread scholarly attention in the last few years.[11]

The technological developments that might lie behind or reinforce the current preoccupation with time are probably all too obvious: the Global Positioning Satellite (or GPS) system, satellite and mobile or cellular telephones, the internet, and wireless connections of all sorts have roots that go back to the 1960s but they all became tools for ordinary people in the 1990s. Hard as it is to believe, the first web server and first web browser, the World Wide Web, appeared only in 1990 and became available to the public in 1993. The new wireless forms of communication have made the experience of simultaneity an even more widely shared one. We live at the beck and call of ring tones and vibrating alerts even more than time clocks; we live more and more in simultaneity, where work is not an eight hour day to be filled and then stamped by a clock, but a virtual permanence of being in touch. In contrast, our modes of bodily transportation have changed only quantitatively, not qualitatively, but

14

more people have more access to more rapid forms of them than ever before. The airplane still has the same basic shape, but its speed and the number of passengers flying every day have profoundly transformed the experience of travel, not to mention time. Airplane travel too aspires for an approach to simultaneity, getting you from one place to another very quickly and providing in international airports a remarkable, if not downright disturbing, uniformity of experience.

Still, a potential problem lurks in the discussion of time's seeming acceleration, which is a process more than a discrete event. Kern's simultaneity, interiority, and even his thickness of the present seem not to take shape all at once, or even at a certain given time, such as the fin-de-siècle, as much as they develop over time, in an ongoing process. True, there are technological innovations that influence our perception of time, such as the telephone or cinema in the fin-de-siècle, or the internet in our own time. But is it not the constantly accelerating pace of such innovations that affects our sense of time most fundamentally, more fundamentally than any particular innovation at any one particular moment in time? I will return to this problem in my second essay.

15

BETTER LATE THAN NEVER: HISTORIANS' INTEREST IN TIME

Historians, too, have quickened the pace on the subject of time. A few hardy souls ventured into this domain at the very end of the 1970s and beginning of the 1980s: Reinhart Koselleck (1979), Krzysztof Pomian (1984), and Paul Ricoeur (1983–1985), most notably. Yet their works went largely unmined until recently and can hardly compare in influence within the historical discipline to the "diffuse, endlessly multiplying studies of sociocultural time" undertaken by many of the leading figures in cultural anthropology and social theory. One measure of the current renewed interest in time among historians is the reinvigorated engagement with the works of Koselleck and Ricoeur, in particular. Within the heated discussions of philosophy of history from the 1970s to the end of the 1990s, Ricoeur's lonely phenomenological voice was drowned out by the cacophony over postmodernism (and Koselleck and Pomian were almost entirely ignored). But now their work begins to resonate more widely, as time itself attracts more attention among historians.[12]

It is surprising that historians have been relatively slow to pick up the topic of time given the importance of work on collective memory that also dates back to the 1980s. Pierre Nora's influential volumes *Les Lieux de mémoire* began to appear in 1984, the very moment when Ricoeur and Pomian were publishing their works. Should not an interest in memory lead inevitably to an interest in time? Certainly Ricoeur linked the two. Yet, as Nora himself recognized by the time he published the third volume (1992), the places of memory had become sacralized, despite his intentions, and therefore were read as forms of commemoration, that is, as celebrations, not studies of the workings of time. The project lent itself to this development from the beginning. Nora and his collaborators focused on the sedimentation of the past in present objects, and a certain nostalgia for times lost had been present all along. Nora's introductory overview began on a note of impending loss: "We speak so much of memory because there is so little of it left." Aiming to hold back the "increasingly rapid slippage of the present into an historical past," his volumes effectively shored up the present and pushed history back behind the wall of renewed monuments to memory.[13]

In that sense Nora's influential volumes participated, even if against the aim of Nora himself, in what François Hartog has termed "presentism," the hostile takeover of the past by the present, which Hartog takes to be representative of our current "regime of historicity." A similar critical note has been sounded in anthropology. Memory studies in anthropology, encouraged most notably by Nora's volumes, so the criticism runs, suffer from a conflation between memory and the old standbys of ethnographic research, identity and even culture itself. Memory becomes just another word for culture. Studies of time in cultural anthropology have been influenced by structuralist, functionalist, phenomenological, and Marxist models, but not nearly as much by studies of collective memory.[14]

So if interest in collective memory did not stimulate historians' concern with time, what did? In the Anglophone world, Benedict Anderson's influential 1983 book, *Imagined Communities*, played a central role. In a much quoted passage, Anderson argued, following Walter Benjamin, that "what has come to take the place of the mediaeval conception of simultaneity-along-time is ... an idea of 'homogeneous, empty time,' in which simultaneity is, as it were, transverse, cross-time, marked not by prefiguring and fulfillment, but by temporal coincidence, and measured by clock and calendar." Anderson puts the significance of this notion in a nutshell in the footnote to this passage: "So deep-lying is this new idea that one could argue that every essential modern conception is based on a conception of 'meanwhile.'"[15]

Simultaneity—in empty, homogeneous time, measured by clock and calendar—is thus yoked to modernity. Instead of time being the fulfillment of prophecy with the end point (the Second Coming) prefigured from the beginning (the Creation), time opens out, encompasses everyone, believer or not, and has no pre-given endpoint. Time becomes a medium for secular life rather than religious realization, and its measurement becomes crucial. Most important, modernity is linked to the recognition that we all live in the same medium of time and therefore need common measurements of it. In Anderson's argument, new print forms such as newspapers and novels helped create this sense of homogeneous, empty time, the simultaneity of modernity and of the imagined community of nationalism.

19

Needless to say, all current historical interest in time does not flow uniquely from Anderson's book. The concern with time among historians draws on many sources, beginning with the exhaustion of the previously dominant analytical paradigms: Marxism, modernization theory, Annales school, postmodernism and post-structuralism, and identity politics. In response, some have turned back to the German critical theorists who had been previously overshadowed by Theodor Adorno and Max Horkheimer, not just Walter Benjamin, as in the case of Anderson, but also Siegfried Kracauer and Georg Simmel. Benjamin, Kracauer and Simmel showed much more interest in the entertainments of mass culture, from wax museums and arcades to detective novels and film, than did the insiders of the Frankfurt School, or Institut für Sozialforschung, which Kracauer dubbed the Institut für Sozialfälschung (Institute for Social Falsification). While Simmel devoted more attention to space than to time, all three wrote about the new subjective experiences of time and space in modernity. A hardy few historians have ventured even further afield in their pursuit of new directions, looking at recent studies of human behavior in the fields of cognitive and evolutionary science. The results of the new interest in time, whatever its sources, are only just beginning to appear, for instance, in two doctoral dissertations in my own field of the French Revolution or the book of Peter Fritzsche, *Stranded in the Present* (2004), which considers the French Revolution a critical turning point in modern experiences of time.[16]

Literary scholars seized upon the subject of time before historians, and they registered the influence of Anderson sooner as a result. There are many reasons for this anticipation in literature besides the fact that Anderson gave great prominence to the novel in his argument. "All literature is about time," remarks J. Hillis Miller, and countless studies of temporality in the works of one or another author back up his claim. Can one think about time without invoking the temporal experiments of the great literary modernists such as Virginia Woolf, Joyce, or Proust? Yet Miller goes on to argue that "explicit concern with time seems today a feature of a somewhat faded modernism," and he even suggests that "Time may nevertheless make a backdoor entry through the now ubiquitous topic of 'history,'" a development that Miller finds of dubious merit.[17]

The "somewhat faded modernism" makes an important point, however inadvertently. Literary schol-

21

ars took an interest in time earlier because both modernism and postmodernism had more of an impact in literature than in history. Once "modernity" and all it implies became an issue in the humanities, time was bound to come up for discussion, for "modernity" is first and foremost a set of notions about and experiences of temporality. Historians tend to assume the existence of "modernity," indeed posit it as a fundamental dividing line in historical studies, but for the most part they describe it in their work rather than investigating its workings as a specifically temporal category. Historians do not generally examine any of their categories of time. Koselleck therefore opens his pioneering book on the subject with this sentence: "The question of what historical time might be belongs to those questions which historical science has the most difficulty answering."[18]

It is hardly accidental, then, that historians of the non-West have played a key role in drawing the attention of historians to the conundrums of time. Historians of the West usually take the modern schema of time for granted because it provides the foundations of their discipline. Historians of the non-West, in contrast, have to confront the nonconformity or uneasy conformity of their cultures to the western model. Especially influential in the Anglophone world have been the insights of Dipesh Chakrabarty, an historian of India concerned with the post-colonial condition. In his influential articles and book on "provincializing Europe," Chakrabarty dissects the habit of writing about Indian "failure" to, in his ironic phrase, "keep an appointment with its destiny." Chakrabarty is dismantling the "master narrative" (or grand temporal schema) that is European history: in history "as a discourse produced at the institutional site of the university," he argues, "'Europe' remains the sovereign, theoretical subject of all history, including the ones we call Indian, Chinese, Kenyan, and so on."[19]

Europe is the standard against which all other histories are written, and that standard is a temporal one; the West is advanced, ahead in temporal terms, while the non-West is backward, behind, failing to keep up. The clear implication is that history as a discipline is therefore inherently Western as well as Westernizing. Thus, in his 1999 article, "What Time is Japan?" Sebastian Conrad asserted that "history as an academic discipline, in other words, was exported from Europe to non-European countries in the process of imperialist expansion." That history taught non-Europeans to think of themselves as temporally behind. From the end of the nineteenth century onward, Conrad recounts, Japanese historians have written their history within what he labels a "temporalization of space," measuring the historical progress of their country against the ubiquitous European standard of modernity.[20]

THE MODERN TIME SCHEMA

In fact, however, Anderson notwithstanding, the workings of the modern Western time schema are not well understood, and some have perhaps too quickly jumped to the conclusion that history itself is a Western trademark. Much of the current understanding of the modern workings of time has come from comparisons between the West and non-West, between the modern West and its Western predecessors, and between Newtonian conceptions (still very much at the heart of Anderson's analysis) and what might be imagined to be post-Newtonian ones. I say "imagined to be post-Newtonian" because it is not clear that we can in any meaningful way distance ourselves from

Newtonian conceptions of time, at least as historians. In other words, much of what is known about modern time comes from analysis of what it is not. My aim here is to shift focus back to what it is, or at least what it has been and what it has become.

Several separate, though interrelated, elements constitute the modern time schema. As a dimension or background grid, it is assumed to be *universal, homogenous*, and "*deep*" in the sense of stretching back very, very far in time. Its meanings are *secular* and *natural* rather than divine or supernatural. Finally, it posits a new relationship to the *future*, which can only be developed once time has been secularized and naturalized. In the new relationship to the future, people come to believe that study of the natural (and social) world will enable them to "make progress," "get ahead," "become more advanced," "make up for lost time," in other words, gain some kind of control over the passing of time. None of these assumptions took shape all at once, and all remain debatable. I hope to show how some attention to them will help us make more sense not just of our discipline in the most abstract sense, but even of specific historical dilemmas.

25

Since universal, homogeneous and deep time have become features of common sense, it is difficult for us to grasp the novelty of the concept, which only took hold in stages between the end of the seventeenth and the middle of the nineteenth century. The temporal grid becomes universal only when one chronological frame of reference encompasses everyone (and indeed every species) in the world. While universality came relatively early on—toward the end of the seventeenth century—homogeneity has always been in question and therefore cannot be dated in the same way. Homogeneity may seem to be a corollary of universal time, since Isaac Newton defined "absolute time" in 1687 as flowing "equably without regard to anything external." Yet, homogeneity of time is easier to comprehend in physics than in history. Newton himself distinguished between absolute, true, mathematical time and the "relative, apparent, and common time" of calendars, which also interested him greatly. As the peoples of the world came into greater and greater contact with each other, it became easier to imagine that everyone lived in the same dimension of time. It was and is much harder to stomach the idea that everyone's time, that literally all experience, has the same ontological weight, as it were.[21]

Our own internal memory systems make homogeneity seem unlikely, for we do not remember everything equally, and we do not assign the same importance to every event in our lives. Narration—the telling of stories—seems to necessarily imply differentiation, for they require beginnings and endings and plot lines that privilege some elements over others. Will not some times always matter more than others? World War I takes up more space in a Western Civilization textbook, for example, than the Saltpeter War between Chile and the forces of Peru and Bolivia (1879–1884). Still, past experience teaches us that historical weight is highly variable (stories change), so the Saltpeter War might well matter more than World War I to a Chilean, and might matter more to the rest of the world if Chile becomes a dominant power. We have learned that the weight of events changes over time. It is hard to conceive now that anyone would overlook slavery in telling the history of France in the eighteenth century, and yet historians of eighteenth-century mainland France largely ignored slavery until recently. It is difficult to imagine a history curriculum that focuses almost exclusively on ancient and perhaps sometimes medieval history, and yet that is just how history was taught in European and American schools or universities until the late nineteenth century. Ultimately, then, we have to accept the conclusion that historical events are much like other sensory information that comes to us; our processes of selection make some events stand out from the background more than others and the foreground and background are constantly shifting over time. What matters most at one time counts for much less at another.

In the background, however, all events are potentially equally present, that is, homogeneous. As long as an occurrence involves actions in the natural world, it is a part of historical time and like all other moments in time. This homogeneity of time becomes important as universalism works its way, precisely because it makes possible the constant revision of histories to take account of the changing world. Our previous obliviousness does not signal the non-existence of events or their lesser ontological weight. We would not have the history of African Americans or of the environment, now, if all natural events were not equally a part of time. In short, the supposition of homogeneity of time creates the potential for recurrent revision, for going back and fishing out previously unnoticed events from the river of time and making them central to new narratives.

Deep time, too, opened the door to continual revision, in this case to including an ever further distant past. A phrase given currency in 1981 by John McPhee writing about geological time, "deep time" refers to the idea that the origins of the earth go back a very long way, certainly much further back than the 4004 B.C. influentially posited by James Ussher in 1650. Deep time only gained widespread acceptance in the nineteenth century and is still contested by some Christians today. Even Newton held fast to the dominant belief of his era that the earth had been created five or six thousand years earlier. Though time was mathematically universal and homogeneous for Newton, it was not necessarily "deep," or, was only deep for God himself.[22]

My interest is not in precisely dating the origins of the earth, the solar system, or the Milky Way (4.5 billion years old for the former, 11–13 billion for the latter, according to the U.S. Geological Survey), but rather in the consequences of this deep time for historical understanding. For the moment, I want simply to note that the deepening of geological time further undermined the dominant Christian framework, in which the creation of the world, the incarnation of Jesus, and the Second Coming could be tightly tied together in one temporal netting that could be fitted over the events of secular life as well. Deep time therefore contributed mightily to the secularization of time in the modern era.

Paradoxically, however, universal, homogeneous and even deep time had Christian origins in what came to be—over time—the Christian calendar. The key breakthrough was the establishment of a universal system of dating that could go as indefinitely backward into the past as forward into the future. In other words, what matters is not the 4004 of Ussher's dating of the creation of the world, but rather the BC attached to that 4004 and the possibility it opened of extending indefinitely backward into deep history (from 4004 in Ussher's time to 13 billion years today). Dating from the supposed birth of Jesus offered an unexpected, crucial advantage; it acted as a pivot on which the mechanism of time could balance with no necessary tipping point on either end. We think of BC/AD (or BCE/CE) as hopelessly mired in Christian and Western hegemony, forgetting that the dating system itself has a complicated history and that its establishment had among its unforeseen—and initially undesired—effects this ability to extend in both temporal directions indefinitely.

The story of the BC/AD dating system is surprisingly murky, given its significance to the modern time schema. AD came first, but it did not appear in the first years or even centuries after the death of Jesus. In 525 AD, facing the end in six years time of a 95-year Easter table attributed to Cyril of Alexandria, a monk from Scythia Minor (present-day Romania) known as Dionysius Exiguus worked out a new Easter table. His innovation was thoroughly pious. Rather than date his cycle in Diocletian time, he recommended marking the time "with years from the incarnation of our Lord Jesus Christ," to distinguish it from "the memory of an impious persecutor of Christians." Therefore, instead of beginning with year 248 of Diocletian, he opened his table with 532 AD. Since Dionysius did not say how he arrived at 532, the reasons for his dating remain a subject of lively controversy. It seems likely, in any case, that Dionysius dated the Incarnation to March 25, 1 AD because

March 25 had become the accepted date for the conception of Christ once December 25 had become the accepted day for Christmas—in the course of the fourth century. March 25, 1 AD had the added advantage of being a Good Friday according to the Alexandrian method of computing Easter and March 25 was also considered by many to be the first day of Creation as well.[23]

The innovation took time to take hold. Dionysius himself had no intention of creating a new dating system for ordinary use. The English pioneered the use of the era of the incarnation for practical matters such as the dating of charters. The oldest is one from king Swaefred of Essex dated 704 AD, but it only exists in a copy from the mid- or late eighth century. The oldest original is a diploma by Aethelbald, king of Mercia, dated 736 AD. Such usage increased toward the end of the eighth century becoming common in the ninth and was even required on episcopal documents by the synod of Chelsea in 816 AD. Bede's *Ecclesiastical History of the English People* (731 AD) was the first historical writing that consistently employed the Dionysian framework. From England the practice spread to the continent, to France in the early ninth century and to

Italy in the late ninth century. Usage became more general in the eleventh century. Yet use of Roman or Creation-based chronologies continued for centuries, even as doubts about them began to accumulate. The precise date of Creation, despite Ussher's confidence, was uncertain, and how could Roman time encompass the new worlds and new histories Europeans were busily discovering?[24]

BC followed AD, yet its history is even harder to pin down with chronological precision. Bede used the expression "anno igitur ante incarnationem Dominicam" [before the incarnation of the Lord] two times in his 731 history of England, but this seems to have had little resonance. "Ante Nativitatem Christi" appeared in a work by a German monk in 1474. Despite these earlier appearances, a French Jesuit, Dionysius Petavius (or Denis Petau), is usually credited for giving ante Christum (the Latin predecessor to BC) currency, beginning with a work of 1627, *De doctrina temporum*, which appeared in new editions well into the eighteenth century. Whatever the precise influence of Petau's work, there is no question that some form of BC could be found with increasing frequency after the mid-seventeenth century. Bossuet, for example, used dates "before Jesus-Christ" at least twice in his *Discours de l'histoire universelle* of 1681.[25]

Competing dating schemes managed to co-exist for some time, however. When Bossuet wanted to date the completion of Solomon's Temple, for example, he offered "the year 3000 since creation, 488 since the exit from Egypt, and to calibrate Biblical with profane time, 180 years after the taking of Troy, 250 since the foundation of Rome, and 1000 before Jesus-Christ." Ussher's *Annals of the Old Testament* of 1650 (English translation 1658) announced the date of Creation as falling "upon the entrance of the night preceding the twenty third day of Octob., in the year of the Julian [Period—"Calendar" in the text was a mistranslation], 710," and Ussher gave the Julian period dates, "the year of the world," and the "year before Christ" dates in his running margins. The English translation of Petau's work in 1659 also gave the Julian Period year alongside the year before Christ's birth.[26]

The Julian Period, invented by Joseph Scaliger in 1582, combined the 28-year solar cycle, the 19-year lunar cycle, and 15-year indiction cycle (a tax cycle in

4th century Rome) in one Julian Period of 7980 years that began on 1 January 4713 BC (thus even before Creation) and ended in 3267 AD. Each year had three components based on the three cycles; if an ancient source gave a piece of astronomical data, such as the position of the moon, the Julian Period date could be computed, thus making possible the collation and comparison of many Biblical and historical sources that had previously been difficult to reconcile. The Julian Period had the advantage of having year numbers that are all positive (therefore eliminating the problem of a lack of "0" in BC/AD), and the Julian day number is still used by astronomers and information technologists.[27]

Scaliger's invention of the Julian Period reflected the mania for chronology that swept Europe in the sixteenth, seventeenth and eighteenth centuries. Scholars from Scaliger to Newton used astronomy, history, and philology to develop concordances of the various historical and Biblical chronologies. Recapturing the charm of the enterprise is not easy, but Edward Gibbon certainly felt it: "In my childish balance I presumed to weigh the systems of Scaliger and Petavius, of Marsham and Newton which I could seldom study in the original; the Dynasties of Assyria and Egypt were my top and cricket-ball: and my sleep has been disturbed by the difficulty of reconciling the Septuagint and the Hebrew computation." As Anthony Grafton has shown, the development of new chronological sophistication by Scaliger and others ultimately sapped the very foundations of Biblical chronology. Could the Bible—and the presumed date of Creation—be correct if Egyptian dynasties could be dated to before the Flood? Ultimately fossils and the new science of geology completely undid the Biblical dating conventions, but the way was paved by the debates among devout chronologists themselves.[28]

Although Scaliger's Julian Period exercised influence for more than two centuries, it ultimately gave way to BC/AD dating. Newton used the Petavian system in his chronology of 1728, helping to make it the standard. Newton said on his first page, "The times are set down in years before Christ," but he did not use an abbreviation; at the beginning he referred to "in the year before Christ" and thereafter just gave the year. The English translation of Petavius of 1659 had employed A.C. and Ant. Chri. as abbreviations. Until the end of the eighteenth century English authors often still gave the Julian Period alongside A.C. in their chronological tables, but in their narratives A.C. or "year(s) before Christ" eventually overwhelmed the increasingly scant references to the Julian Period. As Joseph Priestley proclaimed in his *Lectures on History* in 1788, "I cannot help observing, that this boasted [Julian] period seems to have been unnecessary for the chief purpose for which it was invented, viz. to serve as a common language for chronologers, and that now little use is made of it, notwithstanding all writers still speak of it in the same magnificent terms. The vulgar Christian aera answers the same purpose as effectually."[29]

Though not known as an historian, Priestley helped create the modern timeline in the 1760s with his large (three feet wide, two feet tall) charts of biography (1765) and of history (1769). The first registered the lives of 2,000 famous men on an equally divided scale of 3,000 years of "universal time," while the second traced 78 principal kingdoms over the same time period. Unlike his chronographical predecessors, Priestley insisted on the uniformity or what I am calling the homogeneity of time; each hundred years occupied the exact same amount of space no matter what the density of remarkable events. Rather than address the problem of dating the beginning of the world and as a consequence leaving a large empty space at the left edge of his charts, Priestley arbitrarily began in 1200 BC with the reign of King David.

Like Priestley, most other eighteenth-century writers of history embraced "the vulgar Christian aera" without understanding its consequences. The BC (or AC) that appeared as a by-product of early modern disputes over chronology opened the way to deep time and even the secularization of time. It also led to the disappearance of the very chronological studies that had given birth to the new dating system in the first place. The chronologists pursued a universalism defined by the ambition to combine natural and supernatural histories, reconciling Biblical and secular chronologies. Since it opened the way to infinite regress into the deep past, the establishment of BC made it possible to sever the study of time from its religious origins and pursue secular aims and explanations instead. Bossuet's form of universal history gave way to one defined by geographical and temporal inclusiveness along a secular continuum. Historians might disagree about the meaning, for instance, of events in the fifth century BC, but they agree on the time frame that constitutes the fifth century BC.

The power of a universal, homogeneous, and deep notion of time is incontestable. The notion undergirds Western science, Western imperialism, globalization, and the current vogue of world history, which some might consider all facets of the same phenomenon. It is not accidental, moreover, that universal, homogeneous, and deep time took hold concomitantly with the development of Western science. The Western calendar eventually prevailed world-wide and has become associated with Western values. It does not follow, however, that universal, homogeneous, or deep time is somehow Western in essence, any more than that the idea of universal, homogeneous time is somehow Christian because dating Easter provided a prime motive for calendar revision or because BC/AD refer to the life of Jesus. Having begun as a Christian exercise in dating Easter and reconciling sacred and profane histories, the BC/AD dating system ended up submerging Christian chronology in an even more universal, homogeneous and deep sense of time.

39

Notes

[1] I have found very useful Vyvyan Evans, *The Structure of Time: Language, Meaning, and Temporal Cognition* (Amsterdam/Philadelphia: John Benjamins, 2003). On the rubber sheet analogy, see, for example, NASA's description of the Gravity Probe B mission at http://science.nasa.gov/headlines/y2000/ast24may_1m.htm Consulted May 24, 2006.

[2] For Aristotle's discussion see http://classics.mit.edu/Aristotle/physics.4.iv.html. Consulted March 28, 2007.

[3] See, for example, CNN coverage of the time at http://www.cnn.com/TECH/specials/y2k/stories/y2k.blessing/ consulted May 19, 2006. Richard Landes, "The Fear of an Apocalyptic Year 1000: Augustinian Historiography, Medieval and Modern," *Speculum*, Vol. 75, No. 1. (Jan., 2000): 97–145.

[4] http://www.sbcannualmeeting.net/sbc00/proc.asp?dt'13-&tod'pm for the approval of Resolution 9. For content of the resolution see http://www.sbcannualmeeting.net/sbc00/resolutions.asp consulted May 18, 2006.

[5] Eric Bruton, *The History of Clocks and Watches* (The Grange, Kent, UK: Grange Books, 2002). On the importance of computation of time, especially in the Middle Ages, see Arno Borst, *Computus: Zeit und Zahl in der Geschichte Europas* (Berlin: Verlag Klaus Wagenbach, 1990).

[6] (Cambridge, MA: Harvard University Press, 1983), quotes pp. 1 and 314.

[7] Kern, p. 13.

[8] See the account in Peter Louis Galison, *Einstein's Clocks, Poincaré's Maps: Empire of Time* (New York: W.W. Norton, 2003), esp. pp. 98–107.

[9] Michael Rosbash, "A Biological Clock," *Daedalus* (Spring, 2003): 27–36, quote p. 27.

[10] Paul J. Steinhardt, "The Endless Universe: A Brief Introduction," *Proceedings of the American Philosophical Society*, 148 (Dec 2004), pp. 464–470. On the conundrums, see, for example, Steven F. Savitt, ed., *Time's Arrows Today: Recent Physical and Philosophical Work on the Direction of Time* (Cambridge: Cambridge University Press, 1995).

[11] On Slow Food, founded in 1986, see http://www.thenation.com/doc/20010820/stille, an article first published August 21, 2001. Consulted May 22, 2006. Hartmut Rosa, "The Speed of Global Flows and the Pace of Democratic Politics," *New Political Science*, Volume 27, Number 4 (December 2005): 445–459. Hartmut Rosa, *Beschleunigung: Die Veränderung der Zeitstrukturen in der Moderne* (Frankfurt am Main: Suhrkamp, 2005).

[12] Examples of the recent revival of interest in time among historians include Aziz Al-Azmeh, *The Times of History: Universal Topics in Islamic Historiography* (Budapest: Central European University Press, 2007) and the forthcoming book by Peter Burke, *A Cultural History of Time, 1500–2000*. Historians have written from time to time about time previously. See, for example, the special issue of *History and Theory* in 1966. Reinhard Koselleck, *Vergangene Zukunft: zur Semantik geschichtlicher Zeiten* (Frankfurt am Main: Suhrkamp, 1979); Krzysztof Pomian, *L'ordre du temps* (Paris: Gallimard, 1984); Paul Ricoeur, *Temps et récit* (Paris: Seuil, 1983–1985). Dudley Andrew, "Tracing Ricoeur," *Diacritics*, 30.2 (Summer 2000): 43–69. On cultural anthropology and its interest in time, see Nancy D. Munn,

41

"The Cultural Anthropology of Time: A Critical Essay," *Annual Review of Anthropology*, 21 (1992): 93–123, quote p. 93.

13 For the introductory overview see Pierre Nora, "Between Memory and History: Les Lieux de Mémoire," *Representations*, No. 26, Special Issue: Memory and Counter-Memory. (Spring, 1989): 7–24, quotes p. 7. For Ricoeur's gentle critique, see *Memory, History, Forgetting*, tr. Kathleen Blamey and David Pellauer (Chicago: University of Chicago Press, 2004), pp. 401–411.

14 François Hartog, *Régimes d'historicité: présentisme et expériences du temps* (Paris: Seuil, 2003). David C. Berliner, "The Abuses of Memory: Reflections on the Memory Boom in Anthropology," *Anthropological Quarterly*, Volume 78, Number 1 (Winter 2005): 197–211. See also, Munn, "The Cultural Anthropology of Time" on recent interest in Maurice Halbwachs's work on collective memory.

15 Benedict Anderson, *Imagined Communities: Reflections on the Origin and Spread of Nationalism* (London: Verso, revised ed., 1991), p. 24.

16 On Kracauer I am indebted to recent lectures by Jacques Revel at UCLA. See his foreword to Siegfriend Kracauer, *L'Histoire. Des avant-dernières choses*, tr. Claude Orsoni (Paris: Stock, 2006). Elizabeth Goodstein, "Style as Substance: Georg Simmel's Phenomenology of Culture," *Cultural Critique*, Vol. 52 (Fall 2002): 209–234. Vanessa R. Schwartz, "Walter Benjamin for Historians," *The American Historical Review*, December 2001 http://www.historycooperative.org/ journals/ahr/106.5/ ah0501001721.html (23 Mar. 2007). For interest in models from the natural sciences, see the discussion of Daniel Smail in chapter 3. Sanja Perovic and William Nelson have both writ-

ten dissertations concerned with time at the end of the eighteenth century and during the French Revolution. Both seem to have been influenced most directly by Koselleck. Peter Fritzsche, *Stranded in the Present: Modern Time and the Melancholy of History* (Cambridge, Mass.: Harvard University Press, 2004).

[17] On the influence of Anderson, see Jonathan D. Culler, "Anderson and the Novel," *Diacritics*, Volume 29, Number 4 (Winter 1999): 20–39. J. Hillis Miller, *Daedalus* (Spring 2003), p. 86.

[18] Reinhard Koselleck, *Futures past: On the semantics of historical time*, trans. Keith Tribe (Cambridge, MA: MIT Press, 1985), p. xxi.

[19] Dipesh Chakrabarty, "Postcoloniality and the Artifice of History: Who Speaks for 'Indian' Pasts?," *Representations*, No. 37, Special Issue: Imperial Fantasies and Postcolonial Histories. (Winter, 1992), pp. 1–26, quote p. 1. These views are further developed in his book, *Provincializing Europe: postcolonial thought and historical difference* (Princeton, N.J.: Princeton University Press, 2000).

[20] Sebastian Conrad, "What Time is Japan? Problems of Comparative (Intercultural) Historiography," *History and Theory*, Vol. 38, No. 1. (Feb., 1999), pp. 67–83, quote p. 69.

[21] Newton is quoted in Donald J. Wilcox, *The Measure of Times Past: Pre-Newtonian Chronologies and the Rhetoric of Relative Time* (Chicago: University of Chicago Press, 1987), p. 22.

[22] For Newton's orthodox views on the age of the earth, see Frank E. Manuel, *Isaac Newton Historian* (Cambridge: Cambridge University Press, 1963), esp. pp. 37–40.

[23] Georges Declercq, *Anno Domini: The Origins of the Christian Era* (Turnhout, Belgium: Brepols, 2000), quote pp. 100–101.

[24] I find Declercq's description in *Anno Domini* easier to follow than Wilcox, *Measure of Times Past*, pp. 119–152.

[25] For a general account, see Duncan Steel, *Marking Time: The Epic Quest to Invent the Perfect Calendar* (New York: John Wiley & Sons, Inc., 2000). Of more use in this context is Masayuki Sato, "Comparative Ideas of Chronology," *History and Theory*, 30 (1991), pp. 275–301, esp. pp. 293–294. For Bossuet, see Jacques-Bénigne Bossuet, *Discours sur l'histoire universelle à Monseigneur le Dauphin pour expliquer la suite de la religion et les changemens des empires* (Paris: S. Mabre-Cramoisy, 1681), p. 24.

[26] Bossuet, *Discours sur l'histoire universelle*, p. 24. James Ussher, *The Annals of the world deduced from the origin of time, and continued to the beginning of the Emperour Vespasians reign, and the totall destruction and abolition of the temple and common-wealth of the Jews: containing the historie of the Old and New Testament, with that of the Macchabees, also the most memorable affairs of Asia and Egypt, and the rise of the empire of the Roman Caesars under C. Julius, and Octavianus : collected from all history, as well sacred, as prophane, and methodically digested* (London: Printed by E. Tyler, for J. Crook ... and for G. Bedell ..., 1658), p. 1. Denis Petau, *The history of the world, or, An account of time. Compiled by the learned Dionisius Petavius. And continued by others, to the year of our Lord, 1659. Together with a geographicall description of Europe, Asia, Africa, and America* (London: J. Streater, and are to be sold by Richard Tomlins, at the Sun and Bible in Pie-Corner, 1659), p. 8, for example.

[27] On Scaliger, see Anthony Grafton, *Joseph Scaliger: A Study in the History of Classical Scholarship*, 2 vols. (Oxford: Clarendon Press; New York: Oxford University Press, 1983 and 1993.)

44

[28] Gibbon is cited in Anthony T. Grafton, "Joseph Scaliger and Historical Chronology: The Rise and Fall of a Discipline," *History and Theory*, 14, No. 2. (May, 1975), pp. 156–185 (quote p. 156).

[29] Sir Isaac Newton, *The Chronology of Ancient Kingdoms Amended. To which is prefix'd, A Short Chronicle from the First Memory of Things in Europe, to the Conquest of Persia by Alexander the Great.* (London: printed for J. Tonson, J. Osborn, and T. Longman; and sold by Alexander Symmer and William Monro, Edinburgh, 1728), see p. 9. On the growing dominance of "year before Christ," see Thomas Falconer, *Chronological Tables: Beginning with the Reign of Solomon, and Ending with the Death of Alexander the Great. With a prefatory discourse.* (Oxford: Clarendon Press, 1796). On Priestley and the invention of the timeline, see Daniel Rosenberg, "Joseph Priestley and the Graphic Invention of Modern Time," in *Studies in Eighteenth-Century Culture*, 36 (2007): 55–103, quote p. 72.

Chapter 2
Modernity and History

Modernity has two related definitions, according to the Oxford English Dictionary. It is "the quality or condition of being modern; modernness of character or style," and "an intellectual tendency or social perspective characterized by departure from or repudiation of traditional ideas, doctrines, and cultural values in favor of contemporary or radical values and beliefs (chiefly those of scientific rationalism and liberalism)." The second definition with its emphasis on breaking from tradition has its roots in the European Enlightenment and French Revolution, though Enlightenment writers themselves did not use the specific term *modernity*. The Oxford English Dictionary cites only one use of the term in English before the middle of the eighteenth century and none by Enlightenment writers. It only appeared in French for the first time in the nineteenth century (first in Chateaubriand) and in Spanish in 1905.[1]

Although there is some question as to whether modernity, as Aristotle said of time more generally, belongs to the class of things that exist or to that of things that do not exist, it does function as a category of our thinking, to judge only by the number of times the word appears in book and article titles. My goal is to explain how it came to shape thinking about history. When did "the modern" emerge as a concept and how did it shape historical writing? Of particular interest is the way the modern came to be seen as a distinct, and eventually superior, category of time.

DEFINING THE MODERN

The meaning of modernity obviously depends on the term *modern*, which itself expanded in significance over time. The English word is based on the fourteenth-century Middle French *moderne*, which like the other Romance languages, derives its meaning

48

from the Latin for "just now," "at the present time." The word appears in Italian in the fourteenth century, in Spanish in the fifteenth, in Portuguese in the sixteenth, in Dutch and Swedish in the seventeenth, and in German in the eighteenth century. In the sixteenth and especially the seventeenth centuries, "modern" was increasingly juxtaposed to "ancient," as in the so-called quarrel between the ancients and moderns. In 1694 the Dictionary of the Académie française defined *moderne* as "new, recent, what is from the latest times. It is opposed to ancient."[2]

The concern with the modern grew steadily throughout the seventeenth century and reached a kind of paroxysm in the 1690s. Already in 1590 in English *modern* was used to signal what is "Characteristic of the present time, or the time of writing; not old-fashioned, antiquated, or obsolete; employing the most up-to-date ideas, techniques, or equipment." This sense of the superiority of the modern did not take root all at once, however. According to the English Short Title Catalogue, only 46 books included *modern* in their title between 1598 and 1650, less than one a year. Between 1650 and 1700, in contrast, the number jumped up to 562 titles, a tenfold increase—at a time when the number of books published did not even double. Paul Hazard put it more elegantly: "At first, people were 'modern' timidly, half-heartedly. After a while, they came to look on it as a feather in their cap, and bragged about it, trailing their coats." Hazard dates the change to the period 1680–1715.[3]

Joan DeJean places greater emphasis on the particular decade of the 1690s, during which a kind of "culture war" pitted the defenders of the ancients against the proponents of the moderns. The ancients believed writers were best served by imitating classical models, whereas the moderns held that new knowledge, following the example of the new science, enabled contemporaries to surpass the ancients. More than literary conflicts were involved. The ancients wanted to reserve literary judgment to professionals; the moderns wanted to involve a wider public, including women as both authors and readers. The ancients feared that civilization would decline as a result of this extension of the public; the moderns praised the new forms of popular culture such as operas and especially novels that encouraged a new emphasis on sensibility and psychological interiority. As a result of the quarrel, the moderns developed a notion of progress, though they feared it might already be slowing down.[4]

What matters most is that Europeans came to see a cleavage between the modern and what came before. A sense of rupture, despite the connotations of the word, probably did not develop all at once or just in one country, however influential. The prospect of a temporal break only gradually took hold during the seventeenth and eighteenth centuries and appeared perhaps even as early as the Renaissance with its invention of "the Middle Ages." Are the "Middle Ages" not a labeling device for launching modernity? Europeans only needed a sense of middle once they began to develop the notion that historical time had a progressive direction. *Medium aevum* appeared in 1604, *moyen âge* in 1640, and *Mittelalter* in 1684; so, once again, the seventeenth century seems the moment at which something new begins to crystallize.[5]

Although Enlightenment authors sometimes found positive elements in the Middle Ages, especially when looking for the origins of modern political institutions, most subscribed to the summary view laid out in Voltaire's article "History" in the *Encyclopédie*.

"A new order of things began with the dismember-
ment of the Roman Empire in the West, which is
called *the history of the Middle Ages*; barbarian history of
barbarian peoples, who on becoming Christians did
not become better for it." At the end of the fifteenth
century, Voltaire continued, the New World was discovered and European politics and arts took on new
forms. The invention of printing and the renewal of
the sciences created the conditions for the writing of
true histories as well, which would replace the
"ridiculous chronicles" of the Middle Ages. By the
middle of the eighteenth century, then, the superiority
of modern times was becoming an established truth
and was beginning to shape the writing of history
itself.[6]

THE STAGES OF HISTORY

From Voltaire onward, Enlightenment historians
completed the process of secularizing and naturali-
zing history writing, and more fatefully still, they introduced the notion of the evolution over time of
human societies. Bossuet, like most sixteenth and seventeenth century chronologists, had tried to recon-

cile sacred and profane histories. In contrast, the philosophical historians of the last half of the eighteenth-century focused entirely on the secular world, sought natural explanations for events, and found a pattern in history by which societies evolved from savagery to civilization. These elements did not crystallize all at once. The 1694 Dictionary of the Académie française, for example, had no entry at all for *civilisation.* The 1798 edition defined the word quite simply: "the action of civilizing or state in which one is civilized." By 1832, however, telling examples had been added: "Retard the civilization of a country. The progress of civilization. The results of civilization. Advanced civilization." Only over time did civilization come to be associated with an evolutionary view of history.[7]

Voltaire led the way with his 1756 *Essay on Universal History and on the Manners and Character of Nations, from Charlemagne to our Day* [*Essay sur l'histoire générale, et sur les moeurs et l'esprit des nations, depuis Charlemagne jusqu'à nos jours,* often translated as *Essay on Manners*]. Like Newton, Voltaire did not challenge the chronological bounds of the Christian time framework; indeed, Voltaire rejected the new geology of the eigh-

53

teenth century and so had no truck with "deep time." His impact on history writing was nonetheless transformative. He simply pushed aside the efforts to reconcile Biblical and secular chronologies and stuck with the secular ones. As he said in his article "History" in the *Encyclopédie*, "The history of events is divided between the sacred and the profane... I will in no way touch upon this respectable subject [sacred history]." Voltaire clearly intended to contrast his efforts with those of "the illustrious Bossuet." Bossuet had begun his *Discourse on Universal History* (1681) with Creation and Adam and Eve. Voltaire started his *Essay* with the history of China and India because they were civilized first.[8]

In the opening pages of his *Essay*, Voltaire took Bossuet to task for ignoring the history of the East when writing a supposedly universal history: "This great writer, while saying a word about the Arabs who founded such a powerful empire and such a flourishing religion, only speaks of them as like a deluge of barbarians. He waxes on about the Egyptians but suppresses the Indians and the Chinese, who are at least as ancient as the peoples of Egypt and not less important." Voltaire cut the Europeans down to size, remarking that "when one wants to know something about the Celts our ancestors, you must have recourse to the Greeks, to the Romans, nations very much posterior to the Asians." So though Voltaire refused any notion of deep time, he nonetheless decentered the Christian narrative by weaving it into a world tapestry in which Christianity did not necessarily have priority.[9]

Although Voltaire gave history an entirely secular cast, and refused to follow Bossuet in tracing the role of providence in human events, he remained a bit vague on the question of causation and development over time. He cited only natural (as opposed to supernatural) causes for events, but no overarching pattern emerged in his accounts. When commenting on the backwardness of the regions near Venice in the seventeenth century (Croatia, Dalmatia), for example, Voltaire threw up his hands and concluded, "with what slowness, what difficulty humankind civilizes itself and society perfects itself." He believed that progress took place in specific domains (the arts, the sciences) and at certain moments in time, perhaps especially his own, but he never advanced a theory of historical development.[10]

Voltaire's 1765 work, *The Philosophy of History*, despite its title, offers little that differs in this regard from the earlier *Essay*. Distinguished unfortunately by repeated tirades against the Jews, the book, published under the pseudonym Abbé Bazin, most often traces bad outcomes to religious superstition, theological disputes, and the influence of monks. The concluding chapter captures the general tone: in it Voltaire rails against legislators of every epoch who have claimed that the Divinity dictated laws to them. These laws are "eternally arbitrary," whether they established consuls, aristocracy, democracy or monarchy. Those who claimed divine inspiration acted only in their own interest, Voltaire insists, and should simply be considered blasphemers and traitors. His interest in combating ubiquitous religious fanaticism precluded any concern with patterns of historical evolution.[11]

Unlike Voltaire, Montesquieu was not vague about causation. He cited the influence of climate, the quality of the soil, demography, and commerce when developing his ideal types of republic, monarchy, and despotism in *The Spirit of Laws* (1748). But Montesquieu did not link those types to a developmental schema; they did not constitute progressive stages of history. Still, his attention to historical causation provided grist to the mill of those seeking such a history, such as the French administrator and economist Anne-Robert-Jacques Turgot and the Scottish philosophers of civility, in particular Adam Ferguson and John Millar. Although a developmental history can be found even earlier in the eighteenth century in the writings of Giambattista Vico, the Italian's work had little influence before the end of the eighteenth century. In contrast, Turgot helped make the idea of progress in history a topic of international discussion and the Scottish philosophers identified specific stages in that progress, from hunting and gathering, to animal husbandry, to agriculture, to commerce.[12]

The labels for the specific stages varied from author to author, but the idea of development through stages over time was fundamentally the same. Whether societies progressed from the "rude" or "savage" to the "polished" or "civilized" (Ferguson and Millar's terms), the superiority of the latter was implied by the terms themselves. There are at least three steps in the emergence of this crucial notion of the development of societies through temporal stages. The Scottish philosophers first provided the notion of stages of development, but for them the stages were not always progressive. Turgot argued that advancement or progress was continuous, though his historical accounт was much sketchier than that of the Scottish philosophers and his immediate influence more limited. Nonetheless, by the end of the eighteenth century the notion of historical progress had won many important adherents, both in Great Britain and France. In a third step, the French Revolution then helped consolidate the belief that modern times were clearly and irreversibly superior. Along with the sense of superiority of modern times came the corollary that the future could be fashioned by an act of human will.[13]

The full implications of the stages of history only became evident gradually. One of the earliest adumbrations of the stage model was offered by Adam Smith in his 1762 lectures on jurisprudence. He argued for four stages: the age of hunters, the age of shepherds, the age of agriculture, and the age of commerce. Yet Smith never tried to develop these stages in any systematic historical fashion. In *An Essay on the History of Civil Society* (1767) Ferguson did not employ Smith's particular stages, but he did systematically trace the "slow and gradual progress" of "rude nations" and the influence of "the advancement of civil and commercial arts" in making them more "polished." Still, Ferguson's part five was titled "Of the Decline of Nations" and part six, the final part, "Of Corruption and Political Slavery," so Ferguson thought that nations might decline as well as rise. While his view was not strictly speaking cyclical, like Smith he harbored many doubts about the effects of material progress: "The commercial and lucrative arts may continue to prosper, but they gain an ascendant at the expense of other pursuits. The desire of profit stifles the love of perfection. Interest cools the imagination, and hardens the heart."[14]

Millar took the stage model a step further, but even he only seized upon the full significance of his argument over time. In the first editions of *Observations concerning the Distinction of Ranks in Society* in 1771 and 1773 he referred in his preface to "the natural progress of human society" without any further comment. In the 1779 edition, however, he reworked the preface to make his point clearer: "There is thus, in human society, a natural progress from ignorance to knowledge, and from rude, to civilized manners, the several stages of which are usually accompanied with peculiar laws and customs. Various accidental causes, indeed, have contributed to accelerate, or to retard this advancement in different countries." Millar followed David Hume's *History of England* (1754–1762) in making the rise of freedom central to his account; the penultimate section 3 of Chapter VI of Millar's book was titled "Causes of the freedom acquired by the labouring people in the modern nations of Europe." This emphasis prompted him, unlike Hume, to denounce slavery; in the last section of the book, Chapter VI, section 4, titled "Political consequences of slavery," Millar argued that slavery was incompatible with the future development of social progress. Many of the elements of Western assumptions of cultural superiority could be found in Millar but he seems to have considered all nations capable of making the same transition. "Retardation" or "advancement" depended on "various accidental causes," not inherent racial or ethnic characteristics.[15]

Turgot did not pursue systematic comparisons between types of societies in the manner of Montesquieu or the Scottish philosophers. In his "Discourse on the Successive Progress of the Human Spirit" of

1750, he showed little interest in specific stages of social development, though he did outline the movement from barbarism to settled agriculture and then to towns, commerce, and the proliferation of arts and crafts. Rather than focus on the mode of subsistence as determining, Turgot pointed to general cultural changes such as the invention of writing, the spread of towns, and the printing press. His outlook was distinctly more sanguine about the present and the future than that of Ferguson or Millar. Where Millar worried about the contradiction between the elimination of slavery in Europe and its continuation in the colonies, even in his own time, Turgot drew a sharp distinction between the profound "wound" opened by the barbarian takeover of the Roman Empire and the "resounding success of the last centuries." "Kings without authority, unchecked nobles, enslaved peoples, countrysides covered with fortresses and repeatedly ravaged; war burning between one town and another, one village and another…no commerce, all communication interrupted…. The grossest ignorance spread through all nations and all the professions. A deplorable picture, all too true to life, of Europe during several centuries." Turgot's depiction of the Middle Ages had already anticipated Voltaire's.

Even at the darkest moments, however, the successes of the future arts and sciences were germinating. The towns survived and then regained vigor under the protection of princes. "Different series of events took place in the different countries of the world, and their many separate routes converged finally on the same goal of lifting up the human spirit from its ruins." In this early paean to progress, Turgot rhapsodizes about the effects of time itself: "Les temps sont arrivés" [the times ripened]; or better yet, "Time, unfold your swift wings!" Turgot captured in these few pages the momentousness of the attention to historical development. In 1750 he may not have been entirely aware of its significance, but his own later actions indicate that he soon grasped it: those who could unlock the secrets of the passage of time would be able to influence, if not control, the future.[16]

In another unpublished work of about the same time on universal history, Turgot further developed his notions about the progress of humankind. He put aside his fulminations about the Middle Ages and said more about the general stages of historical development from hunting, to herding, to agriculture, to urban and commercial ways of life. Progress, Turgot insisted, was "inevitable," even if mixed in with periods of decline. Yet "progress has been very different among different peoples." Here Turgot seemed to be taking the fateful step that led toward European and eventually a more general Western superiority, in which the developmental schema is, as it were, spatialized. Some nations in the present remain stuck in their historical backwardness while others show the effects of their historical advancement. "A glance over the earth puts before our eyes, even today, the whole history of the human race, showing us traces of all the steps and monuments of all the stages through which it has passed from the barbarism, still in existence, of the American peoples to the civilisation of the most enlightened nations of Europe." Turgot explicitly rejected Montesquieu's reliance on climate as an explanation for the differences between peoples but he was not entirely clear about what he wanted to propose instead. Density of population, commerce, the rise of scientific method, printing, and modes of communication all seem to enter into the equation. Most important, however, is that all these were factors produced from within human societies themselves and could be studied for their significance. A crucial link had been established, by Turgot and the Scottish philosophers, to the nineteenth-century view (present, for example, in Marx and Comte) that the study of the past could reveal the general laws of social development.[17]

The influence of Turgot's ideas of historical progress from the early 1750s is difficult to measure with precision. It seems to have been recognized more clearly in hindsight (in the 1790s and early decades of the nineteenth century) than at the time, since both the "Discourse" and "Universal History" remained unpublished until the first edition of his collected works in 1808–1811. Turgot was known to his contemporaries, such as Hume, as an exponent of the notion of human perfectibility and historical progress, but his later reputation as a prophet of perfectibility rested mainly on Jean-Antoine-Nicolas Caritat, marquis de Condorcet, his friend and disciple, who wrote his biography in 1786, and Pierre Samuel Dupont de Nemours, who published a memoir on his life and works in 1781–1782 and prepared the first edition of his collected works. For Condorcet, Turgot ranked with Richard Price and Joseph Priestley as one of the three apostles of the "new doctrine of limitless human perfectibility." But Condorcet made this remark only in 1794 in his *Sketch for a Historical Picture of the Progress of the Human Mind.* Still, the back and forth between French and British authors (Turgot corresponded with Hume and Price and knew English) and the parallel development on the two sides of the Channel of notions of social progress through stages of development led to deeper and deeper rooting of these notions over the course of the eighteenth century.[18]

THE FRENCH REVOLUTION

The French revolutionaries were too busy making history to write much of it (Condorcet being a rare exception), but the event itself profoundly influenced the European understanding of modernity. It was no longer enough to build upon the breakthroughs in knowledge accomplished since the Renaissance, as Voltaire and Turgot advised; revolution required a conscious breach in time. In his inimitable fashion, Condorcet explained, on the eve of his own death in 1794, why the French Revolution took the form of a rupture. He was comparing the American and French Revolutions:

Not having at all to reform a vicious system of taxes; not having to destroy feudal tyrannies, hereditary distinctions, rich, powerful or privileged guilds, or a system of religious intolerance, [the Americans] could limit themselves to establishing new powers and substituting them for those that the British nation until then exercised over them. Nothing in these innovations reached the mass of the people; nothing changed in the relations formed between individuals. In France, by contrast, the revolution had to embrace the entire economy of the society, change all social relations, and reach to the last links in the political chain.

This sense of a fundamental break was so widely shared among the French revolutionaries that they reformulated the measures of time itself, dating modern time from the establishment of the new French republic and devising a calendar based on ten-day weeks, with new names for the months and days, and for a while trying to decimalize the clock.[19]

Although many authors, such as Germaine de Staël and François Guizot, used *moyen âge* in a neutral or even positive manner after the French Revolution, the revolutionaries themselves often identified the Middle Ages more closely with "the feudal regime." In August 1789, in response to peasant uprisings but also in the culmination of a long campaign by many Enlightenment writers, the National Assembly voted to "destroy entirely the feudal regime." When Maximilien Robespierre denounced in 1793 the "absurd ideas of despotism and of feudal pride," he was only taking a step further the language developed before him by Voltaire ("Nulle grande ville, point de commerce, point de beaux arts sous un gouvernement purement féodal"), Jean-Jacques Rousseau ("système absurde s'il en fût jamais, contraire aux principes du droit naturel et à toute bonne politie"), or Gabriel Bonnot de Mably ("la monstrueuse anarchie du gouvernement féodal"). Robespierre now deliberately amalgamated monarchical despotism and feudal arrogance, whereas Voltaire, Mably, and even Rousseau clearly distinguished between them.[20]

The endeavor to "destroy entirely the feudal regime" in August 1789 marked just the beginning of an effort to break with the past. The signposts of this odyssey are well known: the destruction of royal statues, monuments, and decorations after August 10, 1792; the executions of the king and queen and anonymous disposal of their bodies; the attempt to popularize new secular names for children in line

67

with the new names of months and new festivals on the calendar; the appearance of new symbols, revolutionary catechisms, even the informal *tu* in French and the universal address of *citoyen* or *citoyenne* to replace *vous* and Monsieur/Madame. Indeed, innovation itself now took on a new, positive meaning.

A new relationship to time was the most significant change, and perhaps the defining development, of the French Revolution. Yet, this experience of temporality could not be decreed, as the devisers of the new revolutionary calendar discovered to their chagrin; it had to be lived and learned. Leaders could encourage their followers to rub out reminders of the past and adopt new symbols as their own, but they soon found that adherence was not automatic. The new calendar ultimately failed, though not for want of official effort, while the metric system succeeded. The revolutionary tricolor, *les droits de l'homme*, and Marianne, symbol of the Republic, all eventually triumphed. Even the much dreaded guillotine lasted. Special costumes for legislators, the Constitutional Church, and theophilanthropy all fell by the wayside. Still, some of the most polarizing of revolutionary inventions—the Festival of Reason, the Committee of Public Safety, the Terror itself—remained in the repositories of collective memory, suggesting that even when the institution of the new failed, the sheer scale of the endeavor itself signaled a rupture in secular time.

In the herculean effort to break with the past, the revolutionaries created a kind of "mythic present," a sense that they were redrafting the social contract and recapturing a kind of primal moment of national community. With events falling one upon the other at high speed, the present seemed elongated. The newspaper *Révolutions de Paris*, for example, in its second issue referred to the third week in July 1789 as "a week that was for us six centuries." On the evening of October 6, 1789 Jacques-Pierre Brissot breathlessly scribbled his first account of the "October Days" (October 5–6, 1789) for his newspaper *Le Patriote français*. "The events that have taken place right in front of us appear almost like a dream." This was just one of many *journées*, days that felt endlessly long when lived through, days whose trance-like events effected major personal and political transformations, that is, rupture with the past.[21]

At the same time, the revolutionaries were frantically constructing narratives about how effacing the past and intensifying the present could enable the French to consciously reshape their future. Deputy Henri Grégoire, one of the revolutionary leaders most in tune with the significance of unfolding events, laid out his interpretation at the height of the Year II: "The French people have gone beyond all other peoples; however, the detestable regime whose remnants we are shaking off keeps us still a great distance from nature; there is still an enormous gap between what we are and what we could be. Let us hurry to fill this gap; let us reconstitute human nature by giving it a new stamp." The Terror sprouted from the effort to "fill this gap," "to reconstitute human nature," or in other words, to accelerate the effects of time.[22]

The Revolution consequently opened the prospect of a new kind of voluntarism, that is, the notion that human will could consciously shape the future and thereby accelerate the effects of time. At the same time, it also cleared a path to a new kind of determinism. Bertrand Barère, leading member of the Committee of Public Safety, and thus one of the architects of the Terror, excused his actions as the product of his time:

I did not at all shape my epoch, time of revolution and political storms...; I only did what I had to do, obey it. It [*l'époque*] sovereignly commanded so many peoples and kings, so many geniuses, so many talents, wills and even events that this submission to the era and this obedience to the spirit of the century cannot be imputed to crime or fault.

Voluntarism—the idea that humans could shape their future—and determinism were two faces of the same coin, as would be shown repeatedly in the works of Hegel and Marx, for example. The Enlightenment historians had shown how humans could study their own past to get a sense of the direction of history. With this knowledge, humans could then decide to facilitate progress (accelerate time), as Turgot did himself as a government minister and as the revolutionaries tried to do on a massive scale. But they could also come to appreciate in a new way how as humans they were mired in time, how they "obeyed" their epoch, as Barère put it.[23]

Even those who resisted the French Revolution—perhaps especially those who resisted it—felt the rift that it opened. As early as 1790, Edmund Burke would comment, "It appears to me as if I were in a great crisis, not of the affairs of France alone, but of all Europe, perhaps of more than Europe. All circumstances taken together, the French Revolution is the most astonishing that has hitherto happened in the world." A decade later, in 1802, the conservative ideologue Louis de Bonald explained that previous political theorists could not accomplish their task because they had not yet seen "the most decisive of all the events, the French Revolution, reserved, it seems, for the final instruction of the universe." Having witnessed the extremes brought on by the Revolution, he concluded, "all the accidents of society are known; the *tour du monde social* is completed; we have traveled to the two poles; there remains no territory to be discovered; and the moment has come to offer to man the map of the moral universe and the theory of society." The French Revolution marked a, if not the, decisive break in human history for reactionaries and revolutionaries alike. Modernity, though the term itself was not yet well-established, was the byproduct of this conflict between proponents and opponents of the revolutionary rupture in time.[24]

MODERNITY AS A TEMPORAL EXPERIENCE

I have passed too quickly over the novel ways in which the revolutionaries stitched together past, present, and future, and as a result my account has offered mainly an intellectual history rather than a cultural, social, or political one. It is possible to approach this subject in a very different way, as does William Nelson, who shows how practices such as animal breeding and economic modeling helped generate a new disposition toward the future in the eighteenth century. Such fine-grained analysis in different registers is critical to deepening our understanding of the seventeenth and eighteenth century reorientation toward time.[25]

In some ways, modernity takes shape as a temporal category only very gradually between the Renaissance, with the invention of the Middle Ages, and the French Revolution, with its aim to break with the past. In other ways, though, it moves by fits and starts, changing little in some respects over decades and then very quickly at precise moments. It is perhaps not very surprising that a specialist in the history of the French Revolution like myself would give a certain priority to that moment when time is profoundly politicized; control over time becomes a political issue in a very self-conscious fashion during the French Revolution. Some support for this focus on the French Revolution can be found in Peter Fritzsche's argument that "something quite new develops around 1800, in the decades around the French Revolution: the perception of the restless iteration of the new so that the past no longer served as a faithful guide to the future, as it had in the exemplary rendering of events and characters since the Renaissance." This disconnection from the past led to a kind of cultural melancholy—Fritzsche's title is *Stranded in the Present: Modern Time and the Melancholy of History*—but it gave history writing a much larger role than ever before. The past turned "opaque," as he puts it, requiring more serious scholarship. But it also appealed to more and more people; the French Revolution brought the people on to the stage of politics, and historians therefore had to pay attention to them in their writing. The genres of historical writing proliferated, with the historical novel being one of the striking examples. Modernity and history writing thus became complicit. By reconfiguring the past, the very positing of modernity opened up a new role for history.[26]

If modernity exists—and I still want to admit some doubts on this score—then it is at least in large measure a category having to do with the experience of time. Reinhart Koselleck's formulation, though sometimes obscure, remains pertinent, and it certainly influenced Fritzsche's as well as my own account. Over the course of the early modern period [*frühen Neuzeit*], Koselleck argues, history was "temporalized" as it became "singular" and superior to preceding times. It becomes singular in the sense that it ceased being a repository of repeatable exempla and became instead a nonreplicable progression. At the end of this process "there is the peculiar form of acceleration which characterizes modernity." Koselleck traces the experience of acceleration to the French Revolution, for its leaders unconsciously secularized the eschatological expectations of Christians. Afterward, however, acceleration only quickened. Here Koselleck's explanation becomes quite general, if not tautological: acceleration is caused by modernity itself. "But since the onset of such acceleration, the tempo of historical time has constantly

75

been changing, and today, thanks to the population explosion, development of technological powers, and the consequent frequent changes of regime, acceleration belongs to everyday experience."[27]

Although Koselleck never says much about acceleration, he does insist that it "involves a category of historical cognition which is likely to supersede the idea of progress conceived simply in terms of an optimization (improvement, *perfectionnement*)." In this he appears to be right, since progress, while always contested, has seemed especially questionable after the horrors of the twentieth—and now twenty-first—centuries. Koselleck defines acceleration in elliptical terms as the "constant renewal" of the difference between the "space of experience" and the "horizon of expectation." If I understand him correctly, he means that as the experience of the past and the expectations for the future grow ever more distant from each other, the sense of rushing to transit from one to the other only increases. Acceleration is neither a product of ideology nor based in "natural time"; rather it is, he maintains, "a genuine historical quality." I interpret this to mean, because here Koselleck is especially opaque, that the lived experience of acceleration is real; time itself is not different but the experience of time is. Koselleck's only clue to what he means by "genuine historical quality" is his emphasis on "technoindustrial progress" and "the acceleration of temporal rhythms and intervals in the environment," as in the time saved by the increasing division of labor and by machines.[28]

If modernity is the product of a certain historical development, then it may also have an end point. In his last paragraphs, Koselleck suggests that modernity as a category of understanding may now be exhausted: "experiences can only be accumulated because they are—as experiences—repeatable. There must then exist long-term formal structures in history which allow the repeated accumulation of experience. But for this, the difference between experience and expectation has to be bridged to such an extent that history might once again be regarded as exemplary. History is only able to recognize what continually changes, and what is new, if it has access to the conventions within which lasting structures are concealed." Just what Koselleck means in this passage remains open to interpretation. Is he calling for a return to Cicero's *historia magistra vitae*—history as the teacher of life through eternally valid principles? Does he regret the defeat of the ancients by the moderns? Does he wish for an orientation toward time that gives more attention to the past and perhaps also to the future and correspondingly less to the present?[29]

Koselleck did not invent the notion of the acceleration of time, which can be found in much of recent social theory. As William Scheuerman sums up recent writings on the subject, "The reason Western consciousness has been preoccupied with the phenomenon of social speed is that Western modernity has probably been the main site and birthplace of social acceleration." Social acceleration grew out of capitalism and individualism, Scheuerman argues, which together fostered a preference for incessant scientific and technical innovation. The resulting acceleration takes three forms, which interact to produce a self-propelling feedback loop: technological acceleration, which is easy to measure; social change or transformation, which is harder to measure but still amenable to analysis (many people now change jobs several times rather than maintaining one for a lifetime, for example); and the heightened tempo of everyday life (the feeling of being rushed), which may or may not be an illusion. "Speed inevitably breeds the need for more speed." It is hard, then, not to think of modernity as a top about to spin out of control.[30]

If there is a question about whether time exists, and whether modernity exists, then certainly one might ask whether temporal acceleration exists. Much of the writing about social acceleration, including Koselleck's, shares Martin Heidegger's suspicion of technology and indeed of modernity itself. Even when the analysis is not Heideggerian, as, for example, in Scheuerman, it tends to be alarmist. The point of Scheuerman's book is that social acceleration might undermine liberal democracy because "high-speed society tends to favor high-speed political institutions" and favors executive decision-making at the expense of parliamentary legality and the separation of powers. Somehow speed is not good.[31]

This distrust of speed is especially apparent in the writings of the French theorist Paul Virilio, who claims that "speed is really 'the accident of transfer,' the premature aging of the constituted world. Swept along by its extreme violence, we are going nowhere;

we content ourselves in abandoning the VITAL [VIF] in the interest of the VOID [VIDE] of speed." The political consequences of this void are truly frightening in Virilio's scenario. "Tomorrow, the control of the environment will contribute to the rise of a veritable chrono-politics, or as I would put it, a DROMO-POLITICS, where the nation will disappear solely to the benefit of a social deregulation and a transpolitical deconstruction: telecommand replacing progressively not only command, immediate command, but above all ethics." The "new technologies of instantaneous interactivity" (Virilio published this in 1990 before the rise of the internet) will sap the utility of the distinctions between past, present, and future and ultimately leave us "detached" from ourselves, from our bodies, and even from "the full body of our being" itself. Void indeed.[32]

Yet speed appears to be entirely relative, a truth that becomes apparent, for example, when you are waiting for a photograph to download on your laptop by telephone rather than high-speed connection. When first invented in the early nineteenth century, steam-driven locomotives seemed incredibly fast to contemporaries, though they barely managed to propel railway trains twenty miles an hour. Reacting to the opening of railway lines from Paris to Rouen and Orléans in 1843, Heinrich Heine already spoke of the "tremendous foreboding such as we always feel when there comes an enormous, an unheard-of event whose consequences are imponderable and incalculable... Even the elementary concepts of time and space have begun to vacillate... Just imagine what will happen when the lines to Belgium and Germany are completed and connected up with their railways! I feel as if the mountains and forests of all countries were advancing on Paris. Even now, I can smell the German linden trees; the North Sea's breakers are rolling against my door." The feeling that the world is becoming claustrophically compressed is not a product of the internet.[33]

Scientific studies cannot entirely resolve this question. Experiments have shown that the perceived duration of an interval of time is determined by the complexity of the task assigned rather than the duration of the task itself. In addition, the perceived complexity of a task depends on its relative familiarity. Unfamiliar complexity accounts for the slowing down of time, as in for example the experiences of the

French Revolution. Temporal compression—the sense of time accelerating—comes from the routinization of that complexity. In general, we might conclude that the increasing differentiation of modern society influences our perception of time by producing greater complexity of tasks, but that complexity cuts both ways, producing either compression or protracted duration. In the end, as Vyvyan Evans sums up the research, "temporality derives not from objective properties of events and the relations between them, but rather constitutes a subjective response to such events."[34]

Although I remain less than entirely convinced, therefore, about what Koselleck calls the "genuine historical quality" of acceleration, there is no doubt that a certain kind of "presentism," derived from the modern time schema, poses distinct challenges to history as a discipline. The modern emphasis on moving quickly away from the past, and as Fritzsche puts it, restlessly iterating the new, leads to a kind of disciplinary reductio ad absurdum. This restlessness takes two disciplinary forms that worry me: decreasing attention to "pre-modern" history as increasing emphasis is laid on the direct and even immediate sources of the present, and excessive concern for innovation. In the nineteenth and even much of the twentieth century, most history students studied ancient and medieval history (and most European *gymnasium* students learned Greek and Latin). Now most undergraduates and even many graduate students—at least in the United States—prefer to study the twentieth century (and what they prefer as consumers determines at least in some measure what they are taught). In recent years, more than half of history doctoral students in the U.S. have specialized in American history and most of them have worked on the last 100 years. Is the historical discipline, one wonders, truly historical any more?[35]

The concern for innovation can be found in the relentless progression of "new" histories (and I myself have certainly contributed to this trend). During the entire seventeenth century, only six books published in English had "new history" in their title. In the last five years alone, there have been more than forty ranging from "Art, a new history, to "new history of German literature," "First Crusade, a new history," and just plain "the new history," whose introduction nonetheless has a rather familiar title, "What is History?" (the title of E.H. Carr's book published nearly a half century ago). The pressure to innovate grew steadily within the historical discipline in the twentieth century. When James Harvey Robinson published his book *The New History: Essays Illustrating the Modern Historical Outlook* in 1912, it caused a stir in American historical circles and was immediately hailed or criticized as a manifesto for a new generation of historians. Articles critical of it were still being published in the 1970s. Will the same be said of the "new histories" of the last generation?[36]

The reductio ad absurdum of innovation in history—that the time between the different formulations of the new risks becoming infinitesimally short—derives from an enduring tension within the discipline about its relationship to science, that key element in the breakthrough to modernity. Science proceeds by building upon previous discoveries, but as they advance scientists rarely feel the need to look back to work undertaken more than a short time before. Historians have tended to follow the scientific model, even though it is not entirely germane to historical investigation. So students are more likely to know the most recent historical writings and to be almost entirely ignorant of the work of historians before 1950 and especially before 1900. I am willing to wager right now that not one of my students has ever read a word written by James Harvey Robinson. His "new history" has nothing new to tell them.

Ignorance of past historical writing impoverishes our sense of the discipline and on occasion leads us to reinvent the proverbial wheel, as we discover information that was in fact already known to our predecessors. I have found to my chagrin that I sometimes only give a more up-to-date twist to arguments made long before me by Alphonse Aulard or Albert Mathiez. But repetition in the name of novelty is not the most serious problem. Presentism, at its worst, encourages a kind of moral complacency and self-congratulation. Interpreting the past in terms of present concerns (as it might be said I am doing right here and now) too often leads us to find ourselves morally superior; the Greeks had slavery, even David Hume was a racist, and European women endorsed imperial ventures. Our forbears constantly fail to measure up to our present-day standards. They are not up-to-date. This is not to say that any of these findings are irrelevant or that we should endorse an entirely relativist point of view. Yet we should question the stance of temporal superiority that is implicit in the Western (and now probably worldwide) historical discipline.[37]

From the moment of its foundation, then, history as a discipline already carried the seeds of its future problems. Modernity and history went hand in hand from the start. In the end, however, modernity is more than a time schema. The Oxford English Dictionary definition, with which I began, misrepresents the most crucial element in modernity, i.e., the reliance on reason as the sole standard of truth. Modernity is not just a "repudiation of traditional ideas...in favor of contemporary or radical values and beliefs." It proposes a different standard for determining the validity of values and beliefs, a standard that is not necessarily tied to any particular value or belief. In this sense, I do very much believe that modernity exists, for the standard of reason allows us to question the modern time schema and even the workings of reason itself.

Notes

[1] The definition of "modernity" can be found in the OED, 2nd edition, online at http://dictionary.oed.com For Chateaubriand, see http://colet.lib.uchicago.edu/cgi-bin/search2t?author=&title=&genre=&date=&word=modernit E&CONJUNCT=PHRASE&DISTANCE=3&PROXY=or +fewer&OUTPUT=conc&SYSTEM_DIR=%2Fprojects% 2Fartflb%2Fdatabases%2Fartfl%2FTLF%2FIMAGE%2F

[2] For "modern" in the OED, 2nd edition, online, see fn. 1. The definition from dictionary of the Académie française can be found through ARTFL at http://colet.uchicago.edu/cgi-bin/dico1look.pl?strippedhw=moderne

[3] The figures on book titles come from a search on EBBO, Early English Books Online available at http://eebo.chadwyck.com. Paul Hazard, *The European Mind, 1680–1715*, trans. J. Lewis May (Cleveland and New York: The World Publishing Co., 1963), p. 29.

[4] Joan DeJean, *Ancients Against Moderns: Culture Wars and the Making of a Fin de Siècle* (Chicago: University of Chicago Press), 1997.

[5] John Dagenais and Margaret R. Greer, "Decolonizing the Middle Ages: Introduction," *Journal of Medieval and Early Modern Studies*, vol. 30, Number 3 (Fall 2000), pp. 431–448. On dates of words see http://dictionary.oed.com/cgi/entry/00309084?single=1&query_type=word&queryword=middle+age&first=1&max_to_show=10.

[6] *Encyclopédie ou dictionnaire raisonné des sciences, des arts et des métiers*, vol. 8 (Neufchastel: Samuel Faulche, 1765), p. 223.

[7] ARTFL, http://colet.uchicago.edu/cgibin/dico1look.pl?strippedhw=civilisation

[8] Voltaire, "Histoire," *Encyclopédie ou dictionnaire raisonné des sciences, des arts et des métiers*, vol. 8, p. 221. The reference to the illustrious Bossuet can be found in *Essay sur l'histoire générale, et sur les moeurs et l'esprit des nations, depuis Charlemagne jusqu'a nos jours* (Genève, Cramer, 1756.), p. 3. On Voltaire and Bossuet, see J.H. Brumfitt, ed., *Les Oeuvres completes de Voltaire: The Complete Works of Voltaire*, 59 (Geneva: Institut et Musée Voltaire, Univ. of Toronto Press, 1969), esp. pp. 32–35.

[9] Voltaire, *Essay*, pp. 3–4. On Voltaire's rejection of eighteenth-century geology and its efforts to push back the dating of the earths origins, see Paolo Rossi, *The Dark Abyss of Time: The History of the Earth and the History of Nations from Hooke to Vico*, tr. Lydia G. Cochrane (Chicago: University of Chicago Press, 1984), esp. pp. 91–95.

[10] Voltaire, *Essay*, p. 231. On Voltaire's somewhat contradictory views of progress, see J.H. Brumfitt, *Voltaire: Historian* (Oxford: Oxford University Press, 1958), pp. 121–128.

[11] *La Philosophie de l'histoire* can be found in Brumfitt, ed., *Les Oeuvres complètes de Voltaire*, 59, see especially chapter 53, pp. 274–275.

[12] Although incomplete, especially on the role of Scottish philosophers, still valuable is Ernst Cassirer, *The Philosophy of the Enlightenment*, tr. Fritz C.A. Koelln and James P. Pettegrove (Princeton: Princeton University Press, 1951), pp. 197–233. On the contribution of Scottish philosophers to history, see Murray G.H. Pittock, "Historiography," in Alexander Broadie, ed., *The Cambridge Companion to the Scottish Enlightenment* (Cambridge: Cambridge University Press, 2003), pp. 258–279.

[13] On the spread of the notion see David Spadafora, *The Idea of Progress in Eighteenth-Century Britain* (New Haven: Yale University Press, 1990).

[14] On Smith's stages, see Pittock, "Historiography," p. 262. Adam Ferguson, *An Essay on the History of Civil Society, 1767*, ed. Duncan Forbes (Edinburgh: University Press, 1966), quotes pp. 74 and 217, and see the table of contents.

[15] John Millar, *The Origin of the Distinction of Ranks; or, an Inquiry into the Circumstances which give Rise to Influence Authority in the Different Members of Society*, third edition, corrected and enlarged (London, sold by John Murray, 1779), p. 5.

[16] Anne-Robert-Jacques Turgot, *Oeuvres de Turgot*, 2 vols., ed. Dupont de Nemours (Osnabrück: O. Zeller, 1966), II : 597–611.

[17] Quotes from Turgot's unfinished work "On Universal History," in Ronald L. Meek, ed., *Turgot on Progress, Sociology and Economics* (Cambridge: Cambridge University Press, 1973), pp. 88, 89.

[18] Jean-Antoine-Nicolas de Caritat, marquis de Condorcet, *Esquisse d'un tableau historique des progrès de l'esprit humain* (Paris : Boivin et Cie, 1933.), p. 166.

[19] Condorcet, *Esquisse*, p. 171.

[20] Quotations from Robespierre, Voltaire, Rousseau, and Mably can be found on ARTFL. For the abolition of the feudal regime, see *Archives parlementaires*, vol. 8, p. 356.

[21] *Révolutions de Paris, Dédiées à la Nation*, 2 (Du samedi 18 au 25 juillet 1789), p. 7. *Le Patriote français* [in order to avoid confusion I have modernized the spelling from françois to français], no. LXIII, du Mercredi 7 octobre 1789, p. 3. I have developed some of these ideas in "The World We Have

Gained: The Future of the French Revolution," *American Historical Review*, 108 (February): 1–19.

[22] *Rapport sur l'ouverture d'un concours pour les livres élémentaires de la première éducation, par Grégoire* (Séance du 3 pluviôse an II). I have discussed the "mythic present" and narratives about the Revolution in Lynn Hunt, *Politics, Culture, and Class in the French Revolution* (Berkeley: University of California Press, 1984, 2004).

[23] As cited in Sergio Luzzatto, "Un Futur au passé. La Révolution dans les mémoires des Conventionnels," *Annales historiques de la Révolution française*, 278 (1989): 455–475, quote p. 469. Hippolyte Carnot and David (D'Angers), eds., *Mémoires de B. Barère*, 4 vols. (Paris: Jules Labitte, 1842–1844), vol. 1: 12–13.

[24] Edmund Burke, *Reflections on the Revolution in France*, paragraph 15, http://www.bartleby.com/24/3/1.html; Louis de Bonald, *Législation primitive considérée dans les derniers temps par les seules lumières de la raison, suivie de plusieurs traités et discours politiques*, 3 vols. (Paris: le Clere, An XI–1802), I: 94–95.

[25] William Max Nelson, "The Weapon of Time: Constructing the Future in France, 1750 – Year I" (Ph D dissertation, UCLA: 2006).

[26] Peter Fritzsche, *Stranded in the Present: Modern Time and the Melancholy of History* (Cambridge, MA: Harvard University Press, 2004), quote p. 5.

[27] Reinhart Koselleck, *Futures Past: On the Semantics of Historical Time*, tr. Keith Tribe (Cambridge, MA: MIT Press, 1985), quotes pp. 5 and 47.

[28] Ibid., pp. 281–284.

[29] Ibid., p. 288.

90

[30] William E. Scheuerman, *Liberal Democracy and the Social Acceleration of Time* (Baltimore: Johns Hopkins University Press, 2004), quote pp. 24 and 22. Scheuerman takes his three categories of acceleration from Hartmut Rosa who calls them "dimensions."

[31] Scheuerman, *Liberal Democracy*, p. 26.

[32] James Der Derian, ed., *The Virilio Reader* (Malden, MA and Oxford: Blackwell, 1998), quotes pp. 122 and 129.

[33] As quoted in Wolfgang Schivelbusch, *The Railway Journey: Trains and Travel in the 19th Century*, tr. Anselm Hollo (New York: Urizen Books, 1979), p. 44.

[34] Vyvyan Evans, *The Structure of Time: Language, Meaning and Temporal Cognition* (Amsterdam/Philadelphia: John Benjamins, 2005), p. 21.

[35] For estimations of student preferences, see Robert B. Townsend in *Perspectives*, available at http://www.historians.org/perspectives/issues/ 2006/0601/0601new1.cfm

[36] I came by the figure of six books for the seventeenth century, using Early English Books On-line. Alun Munslow, *The New History* (Harlow New York: Longman, 2003). On Robinson, see David Gross, "The 'New History': A Note of Reappraisal," *History and Theory*, Vol. 13, No. 1. (Feb., 1974), pp. 53–58.

[37] I took up some of these issues in a preliminary way in *Perspectives*, the newsletter of the American Historical Association. http://www.historians.org/Perspectives/issues/ 2002/0205/0205pre1.cfm

Chapter 3

Post Times or the Future
of the Past

Western notions of time have shaped temporal understandings around the world and to a considerable extent have been imposed on the rest of the world. Twenty-five nations sent delegates to the International Meridian Conference that met in Washington D.C. in October 1884 and adopted the observatory at Greenwich, England as the location for the prime meridian (0 longitude). Among them were all the major countries of Europe, many South American countries, the United States, of course, and Turkey and Japan, the sole representatives of their regions. The Europeans presumably stood in for their African colonies. Although all the nations represented did not agree to all of the resolutions passed at the meeting,

93

the collective decisions made there established the time template that governs international commerce and travel in the entire world to this day.[1]

At least world standard time emerged from a meeting of many, even if not all, nations. The history of the adoption of the Gregorian calendar after 1582 shows how Western hegemony could emerge from an even more complicated and seemingly unpredictable series of events. Named after the pope who ordered calendar reform, Gregory XIII, the Gregorian calendar replaced the Julian one, established in 46 BC by Julius Caesar. It was adopted first in Catholic countries and only in the eighteenth century in Protestant ones: Great Britain adopted it in 1752 and Sweden in 1753, for instance. It was embraced by Japan in 1873, Egypt in 1875, China in 1912, Russia after the revolution in 1918, Greece in 1923, and Turkey in 1926.

We would not now regard the Gregorian calendar as an instrument of Catholic religious hegemony, though Protestants did view it that way in 1582. In England, Elizabeth I's government was about to accept the Gregorian calendar when her bishops denounced it as a form of communication with the Bishop of Rome, the Antichrist. Convenience did not prevail over religion in England for another 170 years. Proposals to reform the calendar in a more international spirit were made to the League of Nations in the 1930s and the United Nations in the 1950s, but these failed to garner support, in the case of the United Nations because of resistance from the United States government.[2]

Not surprisingly, then, the adoption of the Gregorian calendar eventually came to be seen as yet another sign of Western cultural domination. In an article published in 1974, for example, the Kenyan intellectual Ali Mazrui complained of the basic factors that Africans cannot even begin to escape. These include the simple facts that each year is divided into twelve months called January, February, March, onwards to December with the number of days chosen by civilizations external to Africa. Each hour of the day is divided on the basis of calculated units of time derived from alien civilizations. The choice of Greenwich Mean Time as a reference point for determining time in Africa is itself also an outgrowth of alien civilizations.

Needless to say, for Mazrui the "alien influence in Africa" also included the adoption of the Gregorian calendar. Yet, Mazrui himself ended up embracing that alien civilization. He was educated in England, and in 1974 he left Africa to take up a professorship in the United States, where he became President of the African Studies Association, advisor to the World Bank, and the creator of a major television series about the African heritage.[3]

Mazrui's case goes to the heart of one of the critical dilemmas of modern time: even if certain forms of control over time are distinctively Western (and modern), can we—should we—hope to escape them? The focus here is not on control over the definition of time itself, though I would certainly support an international commission to refashion the calendar. My concern, rather, is with history as a form of temporal knowledge. We can never escape time as a dimension of life. All humans endeavor to organize the temporal conditions of their existence, and for some theorists, culture itself is the "system of major modifications of naturally embedded time in the material world." But cultures change, and therefore it is possible that we could develop different ways of controlling time and of defining history, even without endorsing the notion that we can somehow supersede the modern, as in post-modernism or post-history.[4]

IS HISTORY WESTERN?

Without reducing all of Western history writing in the last three hundred years to one of its constituent strands, it is possible to trace a strong association between modernity and history as a discipline. Modernity not only gave history new roles in explaining the past and in mobilizing the past as the basis for the new secular community of the nation, but also became, though not for everyone and not always, the telos of historical development. The stage theories of history helped enshrine the modern, civilized nations as the ultimate end of historical development. But this view of history did not completely gel during the Enlightenment, Turgot's suggestive phrases notwithstanding. The pieces of the teleology of modernity only came together to form a whole in the nineteenth century.

By the time of Hegel's lectures on the philosophy of history (delivered 1830–1831), the crucial step of incorporating all the cultures of the world into one universal and teleological history had been taken. For Hegel, "the History of the World is nothing but the development of the Idea of Freedom," and he insisted

that progress culminated in his time and in the Protestant German states in particular. Moreover, he
expressed the attitudes toward Asia and Africa that
would become staples of the broader developmental
and "Orientalist" vision of world history. "World history [Weltgeschichte] goes from East to West, for
Europe is absolutely the end of history, Asia the
beginning." Like Voltaire, Hegel begins with China
and India because they have the oldest histories, yet
for the German philosopher "China and India lie, as
it were, still outside of world history, as prerequisite
moments whose closing down will finally enable
them to come alive and progress." Until now, both
have "remained stationary and fixed."[5]

Africa fares less well still. China, India, Persia,
Syria, and Egypt all figure in Hegel's history, but sub-
Saharan Africa, "Africa proper," lies "beyond the day
of self-conscious history...enveloped in the dark
mantle of Night." Negroes are "completely wild and
untamed," lacking any concept of justice or morality,
and as a result Africa "is no historical part of the
World; it has no movement or development to exhi-
bit." An evolutionary sense of time did not wait for
Charles Darwin.[6]

Hegel did not invent the teleology of modernity, nor was he alone in picking freedom as its central constituent; the Scottish philosophers already pointed to the development of freedom, whether in politics or commerce, as the narrative plot line of history, and Hegel had read extensively in their works. But he did codify the teleology of modernity in ways that would be influential ever after. Many recent critics have tried to trace this evolutionary vision back to the Enlightenment, but these efforts have been more polemical than persuasive. Katherine George demonstrated many years ago (1958) that negative stereotypes about black Africans date back to ancient times. According to the first century BC Greek historian Diodorus Siculus, for example, "they are entirely savage and display the nature of a wild beast...and speaking as they do with a shrill voice and cultivating none of the practices of civilized life as these are found among the rest of mankind, they present a striking contrast when considered in the light of our own customs."[7]

Only from 1800 onward did the chief elements of a deeply pejorative Orientalist vision come together, as the contrast between Voltaire and Hegel demonstrates. Katherine George maintains that eighteenth-century accounts of Africans are more numerous than those of previous eras, more concerned with accuracy, and more sympathetic to those called primitive. William Smith, for instance, wrote in 1744 that "we Christians have as many idle ridiculous Notions and Customs as the Natives of Guinea have, if not more." An important step toward the Orientalist view was taken in 1799 when a group of French intellectuals that included Cuvier, Lamarck, Geoffrey Saint-Hilaire, Cabanis and Pinel founded the Société des Observateurs de l'Homme. They intended to undertake a comparative anthropology of the customs of peoples and a methodical classification of the races based on comparative anatomy. Although the Society had only a brief existence, its members went on to develop the methods of comparative ethnography and ultimately, in the case of Cuvier (1817), the invidious notion that some races were better suited to civilization than others. Joseph Marie de Gérando, one of the members of the Société, laid out the spatialization of time in his *Considerations on the Methods to Follow in the Observation of Savage Peoples* (1800): "The philosophical traveller, sailing to the ends of the earth, is in fact travelling in time; he is exploring the past; every step he makes is the passage of an age."[8]

This appearance of an evolutionary sense of time is often singled out as the true culprit in Eurocentrism. According to Johannes Fabian, for example, "civilization, evolution, development, acculturation, modernization (and their cousins, industrialization, urbanization) are all terms whose conceptual content derives, in ways that can be specified, from evolutionary Time." In Fabian's view the entire enterprise of anthropology has been fundamentally distorted by evolutionary time and the "temporal distancing it involves," which is "needed to show that natural laws or law-like regularities operate in the development of human society and culture." Anthropologists must write as if "primitive" peoples did not share the same moment in time, even if fieldwork as an activity depends on just such coevalness.[9]

The fault of historians is not quite the same, though it shares many of the same sources, according to critics. Dipesh Chakrabarty's influential indictment of 1992 bears repeating: "insofar as the academic discourse of history—that is, 'history' as a discourse produced at the institutional site of the university—is concerned, 'Europe' remains the sovereign, theoretical subject of all histories, including the ones we call

'Indian,' 'Chinese,' 'Kenyan,' and so on. There is a peculiar way in which all these other histories tend to become variations on a master narrative that could be called 'the history of Europe.'" In short, there appears to be no history outside the Western paradigm of modernity. All other histories are simply variations upon it.[10]

Although it has now become clear that Chakrabarty himself intends to continue practicing history, some question whether history can be other than "totalizing," "a cultural and political liability," as Ashis Nandy concludes. Nandy complains that Chakrabarty and others like him have not gone far enough because they only want to change historical practice, rather than abandon it. "They [papers by Chakrabarty and Gyan Prakash] are powerful pleas for alternative histories, not for alternatives to history." Nandy continues, "In a civilization where there are many pasts, encompassing many bitter memories and animosities, to absolutize them with the help of the European concept of history is to attack the organizing principles of the civilization." History and historical consciousness have to be resisted, according to Nandy. Myth should be preferred to history and a certain version of tradition to modernity. In this Nandy purports to follow the lead of Rabindranath Tagore, the influential Bengali intellectual, who just before his death in 1941 bitterly denounced history writing as exclusively concerned with empires, rulers, and political affairs. "Off with your history," Tagore urged.[11]

The rejection of historical consciousness and the historical discipline does not just emanate from non-Western critics of Western hegemony, such as Nandy. Historicism and anti-historicism have been paired in Western thought about history since the nineteenth century. Thus Nietzsche could pronounce that "the time will come when one will prudently refrain from all constructions of the world-process or even of the history of man." "Das Posthistoire" as Lutz Niethammer slyly calls it, combining German and French, attracted both a postmodernist left and a posthistorical right (Carl Schmitt, Bertrand de Jouvenel, Ernst Jünger): "Bourgeois prophets of the Right as well as the Left declare history to be finished." Yet, in the end, Niethammer argues, posthistory "measures itself against the grand directionality of the classical philosophy of history, and seeks to effect a voluntarist turn which, by drawing on the resources of power, will attain the meaning and purpose that is no longer to be found in historical reality." Proponents of posthistory seek to escape from Hegelianism but even Hegel posited an end to history, famously commented upon by Alexandre Kojève (who associated the end of history first with Stalin and then with the "American way of life"). The Hegelian/Kojèvian formulation was later taken up again in 1992 by Francis Fukuyama in *The End of History and the Last Man*. Projections of the end of history will apparently recur as long as we have history.[12]

Not surprisingly, given the connection between history as a discipline and modernity, some critics also want to dispense altogether with modernity as a concept. Frederick Cooper has drawn attention to several important defects in the use of modernity as a concept. It tends to flatten time and therefore discourage analysis of the conflicts within presumably modern societies in the last two hundred years, while simultaneously ignoring much of what went on before, in Europe and elsewhere in the world. It also confuses certain processes of undeniable significance (urbanization, say, or even secularization) with a particular time period, not to mention a particular place, the West. Modernity also tends to proliferate even among its critics with alternative modernities, colonial modernity, Japanese modernity, Indian modernity, etc. Cooper sums up the result: "The concept of modernity, multiplied, therefore runs the gamut, from a singular narrative of capitalism, the nation-state, and individualism—with multiple effects and responses—to a word for everything that has happened in the last five hundred years."[13]

At the conclusion of his long and incisive review of use of the concept, Cooper comes to a sensible, if somewhat frustrating, conclusion:

My purpose has not been to purge the word mo-dernity and certainly not to cast aside the issues that concern those who use the word. It is to advocate a historical practice sensitive to the different ways people frame the relationship of past, present, and future, an understanding of the situations and conjunctures that enable and disable particular representations, and a focus on process and causation in the past and on choice, political organization, responsibility, and accountability in the future.

This formulation is frustrating because Cooper's use of past ("focus on process and causation in the

105

past") and future ("choice, political organization, responsibility, and accountability in the future") seems to derive from the modern time schema itself. We study the past in order to be able to control the future. At the very least, however, it is certainly clear that Cooper has no intention of abandoning history, even if he is unlikely to feature modernity in his accounts.[14]

Cooper does not look to postmodernism for a solution to these dilemmas because postmodernism relies on the same kind of pre-packaged notion of modernism or modernity that he finds problematic; it simply reverses the sign from positive to negative. Despite its explicit suspicion of grand or meta-narratives, such as Hegel's emancipation through reason, and its hostility to overarching social explanations or ideologies, such as liberalism or communism, postmodernism remains caught up in the coils of modernity by its very definition. It can only aim to displace the modern by going beyond it; therefore the modern and modernity must be alive and kicking if postmodernism is to have a raison d'être. Postmodernism generates its own heroic narrative of refusing modernity even while giving modernity a new lease on life.[15]

106

TOWARD A NON-TELEOLOGICAL HISTORY

The modern time schema, world standard time, the Gregorian calendar, the teleology of modernity and the university discipline of history are all Western in origin, but that does not make them inherently or essentially Western. They are all the products of historical contingencies and therefore subject to change in the future. Moreover, they can all be appropriated in ways that might differ fundamentally from what their early proponents envisioned. That is precisely one of the most important effects of time: things, including our perception of time itself, change.

The most problematic of these temporal inventions is the teleology of modernity, the notion that history as a process has a direction and that its goal is modernity. Some elements of this teleological view will prove difficult to dislodge, but it is nevertheless worth the effort. I believe that the modern time schema with its interrelated notions of universal, homogeneous, secular, natural, and deep time, and the Western breakthroughs in historical dating (BC/AD), calendar reform (the Gregorian calendar), and world standard time can all be redeployed in a non-teleological history. Indeed, what is needed is the development of the modern time schema to its logical conclusions.

If we take the modern time schema seriously, we should push our histories much further back in time ("deep" time reaching much further back than Biblical time), and if we pursue a non-teleological version we might also move away from the ancient/medieval/modern categorization toward a more open-ended sense of the future and therefore a less constraining one of the past as well. I am suggesting that we recapture some of the virtues of Voltaire's *histoire générale* when thinking about world history and global history in the present. Voltaire may have rejected deep history and propagated a caricatural view of the Middle Ages, but he also decentered the Christian narrative, putting it in the wider context of world history. His lack of interest in a developmental narrative now seems more than quaint or obsolete; his "general history" may take us part of the way toward history without a defined goal such as modernity, for though Voltaire aimed to include everyone in his general history, he did not fit everyone into just one plot line. New narratives of universal, secular time may require us to go backwards, looking at past histories and past historians, recovering the bits and pieces that have been long ignored but now may prove useful to our purposes.

A non-teleological version of history would be Darwinian in the way that the current modern time schema is not. The evolutionary, progressive, or developmental view of history not only took shape before Darwin (between the Scottish philosophers and Hegel); it never did become Darwinian, though in the later nineteenth century historians did sometimes veer into the vulgarization known as Social Darwinism. The evolutionary view of history (or what Fabian calls evolutionary time) could not be Darwinian because it remained caught up in the telos of the modern. Historical evolution, in this view, had to be advancing toward a goal and that goal was modernity, whether in Hegel, Marx, Comte, or the many social theories of modernization (Weber, Durkheim, Parsons, etc.). Each one defined modernity differently, of course, but modernity still operated as a kind of final purpose animating the progression. In contrast, Darwinism is nothing if it is not non-teleological. Natural selection favors "adaptive structures," but these are incredibly various and virtually unpredictable, if not imperceptible except over very long periods of time.[16]

While some might argue that scholars no longer regard modernity as the telos of history (and surely all do not, perhaps especially those who study "ancient" and "medieval" history), a few recent titles are suggestive of the strong pull of the modernity concept: *African Modernities; Anglicanism: The Answer to Modernity; L'Aube de la modernité; Asian Traditions and Modernization: The Perspective from Singapore; Andere Wege in die Moderne; Anthropologies of Modernity; Antinomies of Modernity*... and these are just titles that begin with "A" in the UCLA library catalog for the last five years. Avoiding social science theories of modernization does not prevent scholars from continuing to reiterate the telos of the modern. It is quite possible to refuse a strict divide between tradition and modernity and still hold to modernity as a meaningful category. Consider just two examples in my own field: Carla Hesse's important book titled, *The Other Enlightenment: How French Women Became Modern*, or my own edited volume, *The Invention of Pornography, 1500–1800: Obscenity and the Origins of Modernity*. At the very least, the modern and modernity allow us to sell books because of their connotation of being up-to-date. But something more fundamental is surely at issue than just commercial advantage; modernity still provides focus for our vision of history.

Even when progress disappears from the vocabulary of historians, and Eurocentrism becomes problematic, the evolutionary view often remains. In an excellent recent article, the historian of China Arif Dirlik claims that "a radical critique of Eurocentrism must rest on a radical critique of the whole project of modernity." But he does not question modernity itself, only its definition: "Modernity in our day is not just EuroAmerican, but is dispersed globally, if not equally or uniformly, in transnational structures of various kinds, in ideologies of development, and the practices of everyday life." To be fair, though, Dirlik is seeking an alternative to "developmentalism," whereas many critics have simply re-evaluated the goal that structures the teleology. The final culmination of development may no longer seem so desirable—Foucault's carceral society, for example, or Koselleck's constant acceleration of time—but it still informs an evolutionary telos.[17]

111

The slow, inadvertently universalizing and homogenizing development of the BC/AD dating system is more fruitfully viewed as an adaptive structure than as an instrument pure and simple of Western hegemony. Invented for religious reasons and pivoting on the life of the central figure of Christianity, BC/AD made it possible to date history infinitely backward as well as forward and thus accommodated and even facilitated the universal, secular, and deep history that Christian scholars found virtually unimaginable before the eighteenth century, even when they were using BC/AD. The Gregorian calendar, though less influential in this regard, had some of the same effects. Introduced for religious reasons, but also as a way of incorporating the new findings of astronomers, it gradually enabled Europeans and then the rest of the world to integrate their secular time schemas. In the case of England, as Robert Poole has shown, the adoption of the Gregorian calendar hastened the disappearance of the traditional popular festive calendar, tied as it was to the Old Style calendar. Thus, ironically, the Gregorian calendar, initially invented for religious reasons, ended up fostering secularization.[18]

Although the modern time schema linked universal, homogeneous, secular, natural, and deep time to the modern, to the embrace of modernity, to being up-to-date, in fact these changes in the understanding of time took place in fitful steps and not all at once at the cusp of modernity. The adoption of AD extended over many centuries, the use of BC cannot yet be very precisely dated, and the spread of the Gregorian calendar reached from 1582 to the twentieth century. There is no one date at which a culture, a nation, a government, or even a person became modern. Modernity may depend on the universalization of calendars and the standardization of time, but it lacks a precise chronology.

So caught up have we been in the telos of the modern, in which everything leads to the present, that we have largely ignored the history of the very far distant past. Daniel Smail complains that historians have remained "In the Grip of Sacred History." Although historians (and Smail means American historians, and he thinks that historians in other countries might differ in significant ways), like other educated people, came to believe in deep history, i.e., that the origins of humans go back much further than the 4000 BC established by Biblical chronologies, they nonetheless continued to date the beginning of the history they teach and study as if nothing much had changed. As Smail explains, "the sacred was deftly translated into a secular key, as Sumeria and the invention of writing replaced the Garden of Eden as the point of origin for Western Civilization. Prehistory came to be an essential part of the story, but the era was cantilevered outside the narratival buttresses that sustain the edifice of Western Civilization. It was there only to illustrate what we are no longer." Smail wants to eliminate the prehistory/history divide in favor of an explicitly Darwinian evolutionary view that emphasizes the haphazardness of most cultural achievements and their origins in universal brain structures and body chemicals. His book *On Deep History and the Brain* is bound to be controversial, especially because of his advocacy of the "new neurohistory," but whether one agrees with his scientific perspective or not, he does point the way to a much greater openness on both ends of the historical process.[19]

I am not arguing that we all need to convert ourselves into historians of Paleolithic peoples and cultures (which would be ludicrous coming from someone who has spent her entire life focusing on the eighteenth century), but Smail forcefully reminds us that historians have not embraced the implications of the modern time schema as rigorously or consistently as they imagine themselves to have done. Smail's efforts to develop a new meta-narrative based on "neurohistory" resonate in interesting ways with Barbara Adam's proposed agenda for social theory. She criticizes studies of time in other cultures—Evans-Pritchard's study of the Nuer or Whorf's investigation of the Hopi, for instance—for using a clock time standard for comparison. Thus Whorf concluded that the Hopi lacked a word for time and had no tenses in their language. He did not look for views of time embedded in descriptions of nature or work perhaps because he made only one short visit to Hopi country and learned most of the language from a native speaker in New York City.[20]

Adam's main interest lies in collapsing the dichotomy between natural time and social time that is built into such accounts. She does not deny the importance of social time; indeed, she endorses George Herbert Mead's position that all time is socially constructed. Still, she draws a distinction between Mead's view and those of other social theorists such as Durkheim who argued for the social construction of time; Mead argued that time is socially constructed because the capacity for social life grows out of nature itself. The social and the natural cannot be seen as dichotomous therefore; they are continuous.

Evolution, according to Adam, means that humans encapsulate the times of nature, much like plants and animals, which also live by biological rhythms, both in terms of their relationship to the present and future, through circadian rhythms, and their relationship to the evolutionary past. Plants and animals have time and know time too, though they do not have a system of reckoning or a means of conceptualizing it. Time, moreover, is essential to sociality, which is for Mead nothing other than the process of adjusting to being in different perspectives and times simultaneously. Symbolizing, conceptualizing, and reckoning time are all evolutionary innovations.

The resonance between Smail and Adam grows out of their common desire to overcome dichotomies between the natural and the social, nature and culture, nature and history. Like Smail, Adam urges social scientists to enlarge the time-span of the social sciences to an evolutionary scale, not in order to stress "determinist mechanisms of change" but rather to draw attention to "those silent, sedimented aspects of our socio-biological being that have come to be taken for granted." "To accept the importance of our evolutionary past for the present," Adam concludes, "is no different in principle from accepting that our history forms an ineradicable part of our social being."[21]

If history—or the social patterns that required explanation—were viewed in this much longer perspective, the ancient/medieval/modern categorization would lose much of its salience because the ancient period would swell to truly enormous size compared to the other two. Yet references to modernity, as we have seen, are not about to disappear, whether out of convenience or conviction. Even David Christian, author of the ambitious universal history *Maps of Time: An Introduction to Big History*, ends his account, which begins at the origin of the universe, with a section on "The Modern Era." He does not employ the terms "ancient" or "medieval," which is telling, yet his "early human history" and "the Holocene"—the titles of part III and part IV of his book—still march toward "the modern era" (part V) with its familiar chapter titles: "approaching modernity"; "globalization, commercialization, and innovation"; "birth of the modern world" and even finally "the great acceleration of the twentieth century." "Ancient" and "medieval" might be disposable if history is viewed in the perspective of deep time, but "modern" turns out to be extremely tenacious.[22]

The tripartite division of ancient/medieval/modern has been questioned even by those who continue to sow the well-worn fields of the more traditional time frame, 4–5,000 BC—present. Some medievalists try to avoid any mention of the Middle Ages or the "medieval," but this has proved difficult to sustain. It might be a better solution to use "centuries"; rather than referring to the early modern period, for example, we could refer specifically to the sixteenth, seventeenth and eighteenth centuries, if that is what we mean. In fact, using centuries would actually force us to be clearer about what we mean. For some, the eighteenth century, for example, is the end of the early modern, for others the beginning of the modern. Yet the idea that a century has some kind of internal coherence is just as artificial and itself a product of modernity. The use of centuries as time designations only became common in the seventeenth century, at least in English and French. It is part of a more general cultural trend of Western self-consciousness about historical progression.[23]

"Ancient," "medieval" and even "modern" and "modernity" would be less troublesome if they were used non-teleologically, as handy temporal pointers that have the advantage, which they do have, of not privileging any particular mode of history—technology, politics, or culture. Modernity would cease to be the ultimate goal of history, then, and would instead function as a provisional endpoint for some, but perhaps not all, societies. It would signal where some societies are rather than include claims about where everyone else in the world is necessarily headed. There is no need to argue that history lacks all sense of direction any more than one need claim that evolution is directionless. Both have been characterized by the development of greater complexity, whether in social organization or in the progression from bacteria to the human brain. Greater complexity in evolution may have established the conditions for the emergence of human reason, but greater complexity in social organization does not guarantee either the emancipation or triumph of reason. If the parallel with evolution works, then historians must grant that our current sense of where we are is not a sign of the telos of history—and that serious reversals are entirely possible in the future. Natural selection favors adaptation, but it also leads on occasion into dead ends.

SOME CONSEQUENCES FOR GLOBAL HISTORY

Even though certain ways of homogenizing and universalizing the measurement of time had their origins in Western countries (and not always the same western countries, it should be noted), history writing has always been global, not Western. In an important article and related book, Sanjay Subrahmanyam disputes "the new orthodoxy" that "Europe alone possessed recognizable forms of history" and with European expansion and colonization imported "history as a form of knowledge" to the non-West. He advocates more attention to the past practice of writing world history. Rather than endorsing a "global history" that simply traces the origins of present-day globalization or "world history" as it was written by Hegel or is sometimes practiced today with an excessively materialist emphasis, he wants to recover the writings of world historians in the past.

Subrahmanyam makes two critically vital points: 1) "history, and even history-writing, can be found in many societies of the sixteenth and seventeenth centuries"; and 2) "history is not a single genre but can be written in many genres," and moreover, "there are many modes of perceiving the past in any society, and not all of them are historical." "It is therefore deeply simplistic and ultimately false," he concludes, "to divide societies (or cultures) into those that are historical and those that are not; rather, ... there were those who viewed the past historically and others who did not, both groups living side by side within the same cultural complex and producing different texts and narratives." Subrahmanyam does not dispute the existence of modernity or the significance of certain time periods for establishing it. In the essay quoted here, he emphasizes the "major and significant transformation in general historiographical practice in the course of the sixteenth century," but he insists that this transformation took place globally, not just in Europe. There is no need to "provincialize Europe," as Chakrabarty urges, if Europe was always just a part of the world, rather than some kind of synecdoche for it.[24]

Subrahmanyam makes a distinction between universal history, as it was practiced before the sixteenth century, and the new world history of the sixteenth century in which scholars write their histories on a global scale. "Where universal histories are symmetrical and well ordered, world histories are accumulative in character, often disordered, and certainly not symmetrical in nature. Its authors are always tempted to add on yet another chapter, and still another one, substituting conjunctions for arguments, and rarely articulating a clear notion of what the skeletal structure of their text is." (Voltaire, by this standard, would be a world history.) Subrahmanyam clearly has great sympathy for this "imperfect" history motivated by an aspiration to enlarge the scope and coverage of history, and so should we.[25]

Subrahmanyam rightly insists that history writing takes many forms and that a sense of history does not even depend on writing or on a precise definition of history as the content of a work. Daniel Smail also severs the link between history and writing though for somewhat different purposes; he wants Paleolithic peoples to be considered historical and not prehistorical. In her fascinating account of the sixteenth-century Moroccan scholar and traveler al-Hasan al-Wazzan, who was known in the West as Leo Africanus, Natalie Zemon Davis similarly pushes out the boundaries of history writing. Al-Wazzan enthusiastically recorded epitaphs he found on tombs of sultans and their wives, deciphered Latin inscriptions on ruins, read chronicles of African history, and insatiably sought out details of past events that had left their traces in the places he visited; and he did all this before he was captured by Christian pirates and sent to the pope as a gift. It could hardly be said that he lacked a sense of history, even before he wrote anything that resembled a history in the Western sense.[26]

History becomes less teleological when "historicality" (the definition of what constitutes the historical) is expanded in this way to make history the patrimony of all peoples and all times, rather than identifying it with the *discipline* taught in Western universities from the nineteenth century onward or the form of *writing* pioneered by Herodotus in the fifth century BC. This refocusing of the lens is not a "new history," but rather the rediscovery of one already long in existence, as both Subrahmanyam and Natalie Davis have shown. Here, in this discovery of world history before world history, this rediscovery of an "imperfect," relentlessly accumulating world history rather than the neatly packaged new style world history that leads inexorably to globalization, the endless pursuit of newer and newer histories itself comes full circle, showing that historical development is not always linear and teleological but sometimes cyclical and ultimately non-teleological. By extending our notions of historicality, then, we can retrace paths long effaced by the great superhighways of intellectual endeavor (Hegelianism, say, or modernization theory), thereby recovering alternative routes to the present and future.

I am hardly the first to advocate an expansion of the field of historicality. Ranajit Guha, one of the founders of the Subaltern Studies group, has written directly in response to Tagore's exhortation, cited earlier: "off with your history." While agreeing with Tagore about "the poverty of historiography" and "the failure of the genre," Guha urges historians to engage creatively with the past "as a story of man's being in the everyday world. It is, in short, a call for historicality to be rescued from its containment in World-history" of the Hegelian type. Historicality, for Guha, is associated with "what is humble and habitual" and is more easily accessed through literature or poetry than the usual documents of history that emphasize elite politics and state concerns. The ordinary men and women of the Indian countryside, he insists, were "never annexed fully to the statist World-history narratives introduced in South Asia by the West." He concludes by invoking Marc Bloch's work on French agrarian history. Bloch had the insight needed to "grasp the historicality of what lies within the range of everyday perception." By comparing Bloch and Tagore, Guha shows that the problem is universal, not just one of the West vs. the non-West.[27]

Historicality, as Guha uses the term, seems to be derived from Martin Heidegger, though Guha does not make this explicit; he cites Heidegger in connection with everydayness which Guha links to but does not equate with historicality. "Historicality" or "historicity," both rather awkward in English, come from the German term *Geschichtlichkeit*, which appeared prominently in the writings of Wilhelm Dilthey and

125

then the phenomenological philosophers. It is therefore not a new term, but rather one, at least in Guha's hands, which seeks to challenge unexamined assumptions about what is properly historical. Wherever time and time's relationship to history come into question, phenomenological philosophy tends to pop up, whether in the writings of Dilthey, Heidegger, Husserl, or more recently, Ricoeur. Phenomenological philosophers paid much more attention to time as a category of understanding than any of the other major trends in twentieth-century philosophy. Thus it becomes apparent that the category of the properly historical can be questioned even from within Western philosophical and historical frameworks. In perhaps the ultimate irony, "historicality" as used in the phenomenological tradition—and by critics such as Guha—can be traced back to Hegel himself.[28]

Although Voltaire can be associated with some of the unpleasant qualities of presentism, his *histoire générale* pointed toward this broader sense of historicality. In his search for an alternative to universal history as Bossuet practiced it, Voltaire urged Europeans to recognize their connections to the east, to recognize that their history was not as separate as they thought:

Nourished by the produce of their lands, dressed in their cloth, amused by the games that they invented, even instructed by their old moral tales, why would we overlook learning about the spirit of those nations to which the merchants of our Europe voyaged as soon as they could find a route to them? Educating yourself as a philosopher about what concerns this globe, you first turn your gaze toward the east, cradle of all the arts, and which gave everything to the west.

For all his defects, and perhaps even thanks to his defects, Voltaire recalls us to a more curious, and yes, even more humble, form of history writing, even if humble is not the first adjective that usually comes to mind in reference to Voltaire. He recognized the West's debt to the East, and he never seems to have imagined that he might detect history's telos, except that he knows his readers must be curious about a much wider world than Europe alone.[29]

As we renew, as we must, our discussions about the meaning of history and its current directions, we might also take a moment to revisit the approaches of our ancestors among the history writers and try to recapture their sense of historicality. We often celebrate the extension of historicality outwards to other cultures, to the "people without history" in our own cultures (peasants, workers, immigrants, women, children, the homeless, illegals), and to other forms of historical knowledge (films, museums, television, even theme parks). Yet we rarely look at our own professional past and our professional predecessors. This systematic neglect is built into the modern time schema that emerged out of the work of the eighteenth-century historians. They—the eighteenth-century historians—paid for their audacity with the condescension of posterity. It is perhaps now time to shake off the dust that has accumulated around their work and rediscover some of their enthusiasms as our own.

Notes

1 Information about the 1884 conference can be found at http://www.greenwich2000.com/millennium/info/conference.htm

2 Robert Poole, "'Give Us Our Eleven Days!': Calendar Reform in Eighteenth-Century England," *Past and Present*, No. 149. (Nov., 1995), pp. 95–139. For U.S. resistance at the United Nations, see http://personal.ecu.edu/mccartyr/Lodge.html

3 Ali A. Mazrui, "Africa, My Conscience and I," *Transition*, No. 46. (1974), pp. 67–71, quote p. 69.

4 Barbara Adam, *Time and Social Theory* (Cambridge, UK: Polity Press, 1990), quoting T. Hägerstrand, p. 110, see also p. 115 on the modern concern with controlling and commodifying time.

5 Georg Wilhelm Friedrich Hegel, *The Philosophy of History*, tr. J. Sibree (New York: Dover, 1956), quotes pp. 456, 103, 116, 139. I have replaced the Sibree translation in two places with my own from Georg Wilhelm Friedrich Hegel, *Vorlesungen über die Philosophie der Geschichte* (Stuttgart, Philipp Reclam, 1961), pp. 168 and 183.

6 Hegel, ibid., pp. 91, 93. See also Enrique Dussel, "Eurocentrism and Modernity (Introduction to the Frankfurt Lectures)," *boundary 2*, Vol. 20, No. 3, The Postmodernism Debate in Latin America (Autumn, 1993), pp. 65–76.

7 On Hegel and Scottish philosophy see by Norbert Waszek, *The Scottish Enlightenment and Hegel's Account of "Civil Society"* (Boston: Kluwer Academic Publishers, 1988). H. M. Hopfl, "From Savage to Scotsman: Conjectural History in the Scottish Enlightenment," *The Journal of British Studies*, Vol. 17,

No. 2. (Spring, 1978): 19–40. Katherine George, "The Civilized West Looks at Primitive Africa: 1400–1800. A Study in Ethnocentrism," *Isis*, 49, no. 1 (March, 1958): 62–72, quote p. 63.

[8] Here I take issue with the analysis of T. Carlos Jacques, "From Savages and Barbarians to Primitives: Africa, Social Typologies, and History in Eighteenth-Century French Philosophy," *History and Theory*, 36 (May, 1997):190–215. His evidence does not support his conclusions about the role of eighteenth-century French philosophy. Quote from Smith in George, p. 71. De Gérando is quoted in Johannes Fabian, *Time and the Other: How Anthropology Makes Its Object* (New York: Columbia University Press, 1983), p. 7. On the role of De Gérando and Cuvier, and the difference between them, see George W. Stocking, Jr., "French Anthropology in 1800," *Isis*, 55, no. 2 (June, 1964): 134–150. Said gives great prominence to the *Description de l'Egypte*, which was published between 1809 and 1828. Edward W. Said, *Orientalism* (New York: Penguin, 1978), p. 84.

[9] Fabian, *Time and the Other*, pp. 17 and 29.

[10] Dipesh Chakrabarty, "Postcoloniality and the Artifice of History: Who Speaks for 'Indian' Pasts?," *Representations*, No. 37, Special Issue: Imperial Fantasies and Postcolonial Histories. (Winter, 1992), pp. 1–26, quote p. 1.

[11] Ashis Nandy, "History's Forgotten Doubles," *History and Theory*, Vol. 34, No. 2, Theme Issue 34: World Historians and Their Critics. (May, 1995), pp. 44–66. quotes pp. 45 and 53. See Chakrabarty's critique in "Modernity and the Past: A Critical Tribute to Ashis Nandy," in Dipesh Chakrabarty, *Habitations of Modernity: Essays in the Wake of Subaltern Studies*

(Chicago: University of Chicago Press, 2002), pp. 38–47. Tagore is quoted with "sadness" in Ranajit Guha, *History at the Limit of World-History* (New York: Columbia University Press, 2002), p. 72.

[12] Lutz Niethammer, *Posthistoire: Has History Come to an End?*, tr. Patrick Camiller (London: Verso, 1992), quotes pp. 24, 58, 138, 67. Fukuyama had not yet appeared when Niethammer published his book in German.

[13] John D. Kelly, "Alternative Modernities or an Alternative to 'Modernity': Getting out of the Modernist Sublime," in Bruce M. Knauft, ed., *Critically Modern: Alternatives, Alterities, Anthropologies* (Bloomington: Indiana University Press, 2002), pp. 258–286. Frederick Cooper, *Colonialism in Question: Theory, Knowledge, History* (Berkeley: University of California Press, 2005), p. 127.

[14] Cooper, p. 149.

[15] Cooper, p. 123.

[16] On Darwin's view, see the account in Derek Freeman, "The Evolutionary Theories of Charles Darwin and Herbert Spencer," *Current Anthropology*, Vol. 15, No. 3. (Sep., 1974): 211–237. Especially useful is Ernst Mayr, "The Idea of Teleology," *Journal of the History of Ideas*, Vol. 53, No. 1. (Jan. – Mar., 1992): 117–135.

[17] Arif Dirlik, "Is There History After Eurocentrism?: Globalism, Postcolonialism, and the Disavowal of History," *Cultural Critique*, no. 42 (Spring 1999): 1–34, quote p. 2, see also p. 29.

[18] Poole, "Give Us Our Eleven Days!", see especially pp. 137–139.

131

[19] Dan Smail, "In the Grip of Sacred History," *The American Historical Review*, vol. 110.5 (2005): 49 pars. 22 Oct. 2006 http://www.historycooperative.org/journals/ahr/110.5/smail.html, quote par. 4. Daniel Lord Smail, *On Deep History and the Brain* (Berkeley: University of California Press, forthcoming 2007).

[20] Adam, *Time and Social Theory*, p. 96. On Whorf's methods and current views, see the review by Leanne Hinton of *Hopi Time*, by Ekkehart Malotki, *American Indian Quarterly*, Vol. 12, No. 4. (Autumn, 1988): 361–364.

[21] Adam, *Time and Social Theory*, quote p. 166.

[22] David Christian, *Maps of Time: An Introduction to Big History* (Berkeley: University of California Press, 2004), table of contents.

[23] The first use recorded by the Oxford English Dictionary of century to mean "each of the successive periods of 100 years" was 1638. http://dictionary.oed.com/cgi/entry/50035713?single=1&query_type=word&queryword=century&first=1&max_to_show=10 It appears for the first time in French in the Dictionary of the Académie française of 1694. http://colet.uchicago.edu/cgi-bin/dico1look.pl?stripped-hw=siecle

[24] Sanjay Subrahmanyam, "On World Historians in the Sixteenth Century," *Representations*, 91 (Summer 2005): 26–57, quotes pp. 26–28.

[25] Subrahmanyam, p. 36.

[26] Natalie Zemon David, *Trickster Travels: A Sixteenth-Century Muslim Between Worlds* (New York: Hill and Wang, 2006), pp. 52–53. See also Natalie Zemon Davis, "What is Universal

132

about History?" in Gunilla Bude, Sebastian Conrad, and Oliver Janz, eds., *Transnationale Geschichte: Themen, Tendenzen und Theorien* (Göttingen: Vandenhoeck & Ruprecht, 2006), pp. 15–20.

[27] In this final passage, Guha in fact cites Henri Lefebvre's discussion of Marc Bloch. Guha likes what Lefebvre claims to like in Bloch. Guha, *History at the Limit of World History,* quotes pp. 6 and 94. Guha's reading of Tagore has been criticized in Rosinka Chaudhuri, "The Flute, Gerontion, and Subaltern Misreadings of Tagore," *Social Text*, Volume 22, Number 1 (Spring 2004): 103–122.

[28] On Guha's use of Heidegger, see *History at the Limit of World History*, p. 93. Leonhard von Renthe-Fink, *Geschichtlichkeit: Ihr terminologischer und begrifflicher Ursprung bei Hegel, Haym, Dilthey und Yorck* (Göttingen: Vandenhoeck und Ruprecht, 1968). Ricoeur provides a brief discussion of Heidegger's use of the term, *Time and Narrative*, vol. 1, tr. Kathleen McLaughlin and David Pellauer (Chicago: University of Chicago Press, 1984), esp. pp. 62–63. See also Harold N. Tuttle, *The Dawn of Historical Reason: The Historicality of Human Existence in the Thought of Dilthey, Heidegger, and Ortegy y Gasset* (New York: Peter Lang, 1994) and Gerhard Bauer, *"Geschichtlichkeit"— Wege und Irrwege eines Begriss* (Berlin: Walter de Gruyter and Co., 1963).

[29] Voltaire, *Essay*, p. 3.

Index